THE NEW ZEALAND POLICEMAN

THE NEW ZEALAND POLICEMAN

The Developing Role of New Zealand Police

By

J. F. GLYNN

1975

Wellington—New Zealand Institute of
Public Administration

PRINTED BY
WRIGHT & CARMAN LIMITED
TRENTHAM

Contents

Acknowledgements

I wish to express my gratitude to the New Zealand Police Department for providing me with the opportunity to study at Victoria University, where this essay was written. I gratefully acknowledge the valuable suggestions made by Neil Cameron (Lecturer in Law at Victoria University of Wellington), Peter Jones (formerly Senior Lecturer in Public Administration at Victoria University), Alistair Paterson (Dean of General Studies, New Zealand Police), and Francis Wogan.

J. F. G.
Wellington
February 1975

The opinions expressed in this essay are the author's, and do not necessarily reflect those of the New Zealand Police Department.

Foreword

In these times of rapid social change, many of our institutions are coming under searching examination and the police are not excluded. In line with other organisations we are endeavouring to anticipate such changes by self-examination and appraisal, and this essay by a perceptive police officer indicates the direction in which we appear to be travelling. I have been closely associated with the many wide sweeping alterations to the police structure over the past decade or so and it is with a great deal of pleasure that I find my staff continuing to give thought to the changes that lie ahead.

I commend this essay to those wishing to add to their store of knowledge of previously unpublished aspects of the police of New Zealand. Chief Inspector Glynn is to be congratulated on a concise and well documented piece of constructive writing.

Commissioner of Police

Introduction

*Always know who you are, where
you are, and what you are doing
there.*[1]

This succinct advice was once offered to young policemen. If
we add another piece of idealism: "Also keep an eye on where
you are going", the basic theme of this essay is laid. What follows
is broadly directed towards those ends—ends which are never
absolutely clear, but which are ends just the same. "It is better
to steer toward a light, however distant, than to steer in total
darkness."[2]

More particularly, the essential area of concern will be the
developing role of the New Zealand police within the social
framework of a changing democratic society. There are several
reasons for selecting this subject for study.

First, despite the very central and conspicuous position of
the police institution in modern life, I can find no evidence of
any attempt by policemen themselves, social scientists, or others
to systematically and rigorously analyse the role of the New
Zealand police. Indeed, in the period from 1938 to 1972 only
one article concerned with the police was published in the *New
Zealand Journal of Public Administration,* while New Zealand
sociological and political science journals have consistently
neglected the police as a subject for study.

[1] V. G. Stretcher, *The Environment of Law Enforcement* (N.J.: Prentice-
Hall, Inc. 1971), p. 92.
[2] R. C. Martin, *Grass Roots* (University of Alabama Press, 1964), p. 88.

9

Where occasional references to the New Zealand police role have been made in other New Zealand publications (e.g. law journals), these have been superficial. The tendency has been to see police in a microscopic, rather than macroscopic light. "To understand the influence of a position or behaviour, we need to relate it not only to the personalities of the occupants and to the network of reciprocal positions with which it is connected, but also to the larger community and society structures within which it operates."[3]

This lack of analysis of the New Zealand police role leads to a plethora of "experts", while unsupported assumptions become accepted as Gospel, and much prejudice tends to be seen as sound common sense.

Why this historical neglect has existed is not clear. Some overseas writers have suggested that the police role in all its complexity is an indefinable concept, mainly because the policeman represents so many different things to so many people who tend to judge police actions by the standard of their own self-interest. This prompted one writer[4] to describe the policeman as "a 'Rorschach' in uniform" clothed "in a mantle of symbolism that stimulates fantasy and projection". Still, one would think that this lack of agreement, which leads to difficulties for policemen trying to carry out the role, should, in itself, present a research challenge to New Zealand social and behavioural scientists.

The second reason for undertaking this study is that currently—specifically since the late 1960s—police are finding themselves caught in a period of unusual uncertainty. Policemen are anxious to clarify their role. One can only generalise as to why this clarification is now so eagerly sought. After all, police have traditionally accepted the ineptitude of the law to define the police role in clear terms.

It is true however that in today's society of rapidly changing

---

[3] Quoted by R. H. Ward in "The Police Role: A Case of Diversity", *The Journal of Criminal Law, Criminology and Police Science*, Vol. 61, No. 4, 1971, p. 584.

[4] Arthur Niederhoffer, *Behind the Shield: The Police in Urban Society* (N.Y.: Doubleday & Co. Ltd, 1967), p. 1.

social values self-doubt is not a phenomenon peculiar only to the police. Police, however, more so perhaps than any other occupational group, achieve an increased prominence in a time of rising social awareness in the community.

Third, there is a need to understand the police role, because the way in which both the police themselves and the public perceive it is crucial to the nature of the on-going functional relationship between the two. If these perceptions are brought into the open, examined and discussed so that they may be mutually and sympathetically understood, then a healthier, more explicitly defined and agreed upon relationship may result. Conversely, if the policeman's concept of his role is different from that of society as a whole, or sections of that society, tension is almost inevitable.

Lastly, being a policeman myself, I feel a need both to express a personal point of view concerning many aspects of the police role and to expose a variety of problems. These problems are not for the police alone to think about. Rather they are society's problems. A policeman, however, is ideally placed to identify many of them. I offer no panacea, nor do I suggest that there are simple solutions. I taken Condliffe's approach. He said that the purpose of an essay "is not so much to solve problems as to raise issues, not to close questions but to open them. . . ."[5]

Above all, I see the value of police themselves taking the initiative in exposing problems. This can motivate others to adopt a scholarly and research-based interest in finding publicly acceptable solutions. Indeed, one of the principal virtues of a society with democratic values is the obligation police in that society may feel for self-analysis and improvement.

It is reasonable to assume too that as our society becomes progressively more complex, problems for the police will multiply correspondingly. In this situation, it would be irresponsible for the police to try to "go it alone", or wait for "outsiders" to resurrect and spotlight problems. One can speculate that to some extent this is the type of inaction which has subjected the

---

[5] J. B. Condliffe, *The Economic Outlook for New Zealand* (Christchurch: Whitcombe and Tombs Ltd, 1969), p. 1.

American police to considerable public odium and which is reflected in the avalanche of beratement and anti-police sentiment published in literature that has reached the New Zealand public and particularly the New Zealand universities. In the absence of authentic New Zealand-produced material on the New Zealand police, to counteract the influence of the American flow, one can surmise that, at least in the minds of the less discerning New Zealand young and not-so-young adults, New Zealand policemen are seen to be subject to the same alleged sins as their American counterparts.

In alluding to the lack of public understanding of the police role in a free society, the noted American police administrator, O. W. Wilson, made this pertinent comment: "These misunderstandings continue unabated because the police are not a vocal scholarly group that devotes much time to presenting in a favourable light the facts that bear on the problem. The literature in consequence is principally devoted to the case against the police; little has been written in their defence. The press, the literature, and even case law are all directed at incidents that discredit the police. . . . Information on which a fairer judgment might be based is not generally circulated."[6]

In brief, what this study may hopefully achieve is:

—To describe the changing social environment in which New Zealand policemen operate and the implications which such an environment has for police work.

—To provide a stimulus for future attempts at greater accuracy in analysing community responsibility for maintaining law and order.

—To provide a fresh dimension to judgments and perspectives on the police role and particularly to shed some light on its diversity, social, and discretionary nature.

—To serve as a source of descriptive and theoretical material on the police role, as well as clarifying a number of issues in a field where there is much confusion.

---

[6] O. W. Wilson, "Police Arrest Privileges in a Free Society", in Sowle, ed., Police Power and Individual Freedom, (Chicago: Aldine Publishing Co., 1962) pp. 25-26.

—To portray a total impression of the police role within the framework of a changing democratic society.

—To restate, in a more realistic way, the broad functional police role in New Zealand.

Throughout this study, I have drawn on overseas studies of the police which, though based on similar but still different cultural and political settings, allow frequent parallels with New Zealand policing and exploration of many issues which are relevant here. Although many aspects of overseas police experience in democratic countries do seem to apply here, I have been mindful of the need to resist the temptation to draw parallels too hastily and in all respects.

1

Some Aspects of Social Change and its Implications for Police

The dynamics of the changing social scene are forcing a complete reassessment of the New Zealand police. Deep-seated changes in attitude and philosophy are taking place within the police, and one should not be misled by the smallness of the visible effects of such changes. The police institution, like any other institution, is not permitted, nor can it afford, to isolate itself from its environment. Let us look briefly at some of the wider social changes pervading society as well as some of the implications these have for the police role.

New Zealand's freedom from severely explosive social issues and its geographic isolation have by no means isolated it from the world-wide changes in the social, environmental and political climate. Cross-cultural contacts in the modern world of swift travel and communications has meant that social change is able to spread rapidly and become internationally contagious.

Conditions, ways of thinking, knowledge itself, attitudes and pace of life—all these have changed swiftly and dramatically. Statements, definitions, accepted ways of doing things are no longer accepted at face value. The immediate reaction is to question, discuss, examine, argue and criticise.

Clearly, these trends are manifested in the values and attitudes of many young New Zealanders who are questioning what they call outmoded laws regarding sex, censorship, obscenity, and so on.

14

Ramsay Clark's words are worth reflecting on: "Being young was never easy. Today it is harder than ever. The confusion, complexity and irrationality of modern mass urban society provide the adolescent with few solid bases for understanding his environment and what it all means. There has been more change between the birth of a father and the birth of a son than in the preceding millennium. . . . The young seek to know themselves in a world permeated with noise, pollution, movement, communication, strangers and gadgets of great complexity.[1]

"The young generation who have grown up since the war are no longer certain it is possible to say what is right or wrong."[2]

Today, "The Temporary Society" is a popular expression. Mosher[3] uses the term in this sense: ". . . The society is temporary in that it is widely known and appreciated that it is changing rapidly and will, in effect, be transformed into another society within a relatively short span of years, say 10 or 15. . . . The parent of the '70's is preparing his infant offspring for a society not the same as his own and not even once removed from his own. It is more nearly twice removed. . . . Few professionals can now claim total competence to handle basic problems even within those functional areas in which they once were recognized as exclusive monopolists. This is a product of growing functional interdependence, which is entirely comparable to the growing geographic interdependence . . . and of the external effects—both costs and benefits—of actions taken in one field upon others. . . . *Crime is no longer a problem for the police alone* nor health for doctors alone nor highways for engineers alone nor justice for lawyers alone."

A few years ago, Sir Dove-Meyer Robinson, Mayor of the largest Polynesian city, gave a book to each of the newly elected councillors as a preparation for their new responsibilities. He asked them to carry out this preparation with a diligence that

[1] R. Clark, *Crime in America* (New York: Simon & Schuster, 1970), pp. 245-249.
[2] Ben Whitaker, *The Police* (London: Eyre & Spottiswoode, 1964), p. 210.
[3] F. C. Mosher, "The Public Service in the Temporary Society," *Public Administration Review* (January-February, 1971), pp. 47-48.

should make them collectively "New Zealand's best informed council". The book was Alvin Toffler's best seller *Future Shock*.[4] The author's main theme is that urban societies in most of the world are experiencing change at so rapid a pace that man's capacity to adapt is at high risk. He may become a victim of future shock, the disease of change.

Toffler believes that society is undergoing a crisis with three key effects. First, the pace of change has been accelerating beyond control so that we have been forced to abbreviate our relationships with other people, buildings, objects and places. Second, rapid change has led to a high level of unpredictability in people's lives. The third feature which Toffler emphasises is the shift from a conformist society to one of high diversification and over-choice, particularly in publications, art, education and in the general market place. In total, Toffler describes how the changing social scene means that jobs are changed more quickly, homes moved, fashions adopted and discarded, knowledge gained and outdated, ideas created and used up faster and faster; marriage, possessions and information become increasingly temporary; sub-cults and ways of living become more diverse—all of which makes people disorientated.

What has been said so far, probably over-dramatises the intensity and implications of change. "Social change is not a uniquely modern phenomenon. Some kinds and degrees of change are universal in human experience. The speed of contemporary change is not totally illusory but it can be exaggerated. . . ."[5] Even allowing for some exaggeration, what does the current rate of change mean for policemen?

Over 3,000 New Zealand policemen form an occupational group which has gained a reputation, imagined or otherwise, among many people for its resistance to change. To state the obvious, all human beings resist or fear change in some way or other. There are many psychological reasons for this. Perhaps the explanation which offers most is Schein's:[6] "Any change in

---

[4] A. Toffler, *Future Shock* (London: The Bodley Head Ltd, 1970).
[5] W. E. Moore, *Social Change* (Prentice Hall, Inc., 1963), p. 1.
[6] Warren G. Bennis *et al.* (eds.), *The Planning of Change* (New York: Holt, Rinehart and Winston, Inc., 1969), p. 99.

behaviour or attitude . . . tends to be emotionally resisted because even the possibility of change implies that previous behaviour and attitude were somehow wrong or inadequate, a conclusion which the change target would be motivated to reject". "The mind likes a new idea as little as the body likes a strange protein, and resists it with similar energy. It would not perhaps be too fanciful to say that a new idea is the most quickly acting antigen known to science. If we watch ourselves honestly we shall often find that we have begun to argue against a new idea even before it has been completely stated . . . I have no doubt that the last statement has already met with some repudiation—and shown how quickly the defence mechanism gets to work."[7]

Probably, any healthy living system will resist change because its life depends to some extent on its ability to establish a steady state. Some of the resistance to change can be healthy; the problem is one of recognising when resistance is of such an order as to inhibit necessary change and when it must be modified or broken. One of the important tasks of leadership is to make this decision.

To suggest however that New Zealand police are over-resistant to change is not supported by the facts. It is not my intention here to catalogue the totality of recent police responses to change. But when one considers the recent surveys plus implementation thrust within the police department in such areas as manpower deployment, training and education, buildings and equipment, new systems of policing, and the creation of new sections to meet special community needs, it is clear that more police advances have been made in the last decade or less, than in the previous seven decades. Even so, this effort has really been a case of running in order to stand still.

How does a police service plan and adapt itself to accommodate a problem which the Commissioner of Police expressed in this way? "The need to be aware of, but not even appear to repress human rights or civil liberties, to be conscious of, but not appear to frustrate sociological drives, to be understanding of liberal philosophies, to be tolerant in the face of group intolerance, to

---

[7] Quoted from a source unknown by G. P. Rabey, "Change and the Older Worker," *N.Z.J.P.A.* (Vol. 34, No. 2), March 1972, p. 35.

be capable of comprehending the issues of academic argument, to remain unbiased in respect to radical action or unreasoned clamour—all these needs must be satisfied by policemen in an endeavour to meet the expectations and demands of a community anxious to retain the comfort and 'status quo' of former times. Yet the police must accomplish this in a new climate so dramatically attuned to the demands for reform and change."[8]

The problem of balancing the desirability of individual freedom against the communal need for order is not resolved—assuming that it can be in a democratic society—by relying solely on the law, which is the last ditch or furthest back defence. Even so, during earlier decades, police were able to draw much of their authority to act from the law, even though it may not have been designed to cover the era of the "clip around the ear" (a period which is never defined!).

Now, we see that the individual seems to be influenced less by laws, religious doctrine, or what the various publics think, than was formerly the case. Public morality is less commonly shared than in the past.

Today's policeman must look constantly to public opinion and he is forced to adjust his attitudes and his actions towards the needs of a changing social climate—this being the new source of legitimation for his authority and acceptance. Power-with rather than power-over is the modern dictum. It is not possible now "to go by the book". "He (the policeman) is no longer simply a law enforcer," writes an English M.P. "He is required to be a social diagnostician, to comprehend the new society of which he is a part and make the right responses to its aberrations."[9]

It is no longer sufficient for the police leader to say that his men acted within their legal powers. Police actions must be, and seen to be, humane. The police leader must be able to justify himself in an encounter with the mass media. People who hold power have new opportunities via the mass media to explain

---

[8] Report of the New Zealand Police Department for the year ended 31 March 1972 (Wellington: Government Printer), p. 5.
[9] Editorial, *The Evening Post,* 10 October 1971.

how they use it. If the explanations are accepted they obtain the quality of authority.

The interesting paradox is that, while most people are not overawed by the law, they still tend to rely heavily on it as a means of controlling anti-social conduct. They are turning in increasing numbers to the police for help, in trying to cope with social problems. This means that the front-line police of today are playing the role of general emergency, human service agents in urban communities. Cast in this role, policemen are increasingly expected to exercise wise discretion, sociological, psychological and even didactic skills in coping with the effects of complex and diverse social problems ranging from resolving family disputes to keeping peace at political demonstrations.

They must now understand and try to alleviate problems concerned with racial prejudice, minority conflict, gang warfare, drug addiction, and child neglect.

Among all those who need a keen perception of change, the policeman occupies the front row. So often these days he operates where the confrontations are taking place—in the middle of the control-freedom dilemma. ". . . The police are the vehicle by which the limits, boundaries, and permissibility of social tolerance are tested."[10]

The community expects the policeman to keep order but cannot tell him how to define "disorder". He must go on representing "law" and "order" even when both seem to have lost their basis in morality and are often in conflict. These are situations when non-enforcement of certain laws may actually contribute to the peace, e.g. at the scene of a demonstration. During his initial training, he learns a set of ground rules and soon finds that many of these no longer seem to apply.

It is not surprising then that many policemen express some confusion at the rate and nature of change confronting them. In a very real sense, their roles are undermined by great shifts in social values and life styles.

[10] A. S. Blumberg and A. Niederhoffer, *The Police in Social and Historical Perspective, The Ambivalent Force: Perspectives on the Police* (New York: Ginn & Co., 1970), p. 7.

One of the essential characteristics of a police service in a democratic society is its capacity to adapt in a reasonable, flexible and imaginative way to changing times. This does not mean that police should allow themselves to be swayed by sudden gusts of popular opinion; nor should they adopt a posture of self-pity by assuming they are the only group affected by social change. Rather they must accept that changes in society are inevitable, are multiplying, but are certainly not always disruptive or undesirable. Many of the changes occurring in society have deep humanitarian motives and have brought desirable demands for more accountability at all levels of society. Policemen must accept that the very substantial changes occurring in society need to be reflected in equally substantial changes in their views about how law and order are maintained; in how they define the modern police role; in how they use their discretion, and in how they think police effectiveness is judged in a democratic society. In other words, policemen must meet change with change.

2

Maintaining Law and Order: How Maintained? Whose Responsibility and Why?

To provide a base there is a need to identify the statutory responsibilities of the police. These have not been defined except in vague and somewhat misleading terms: certainly they do not reflect the diversity of police work.

Each new police entrant is required to take an oath "to see and cause Her Majesty's peace to be kept and preserved . . . and prevent . . . all offences against the peace." The Police Regulations say that each constable "shall be on the alert for the prevention and detection of crime and the protection of the public" and that an officer in charge of a police district "shall be responsible for the general preservation of the peace and order in his district, the prevention of offences and the detection of offenders." To these is added the traditional but uncodified responsibility of "protecting life and property."

In brief then, the traditional standard list of police responsibilities consists of the following:

Prevention and detection of offences
Preservation of peace and good order
Protection of life and property.

With the passage of time these responsibilities have collectively taken on a popular semantic variation, that of "maintaining law and order", or—to use the American idiom—"law enforcement".

What does "law and order" mean? The word "order" is value-impregnated and can mean as much or as little as one wants it to mean. Ward and Woods,[1] in their book *Law and Order in Australia,* claim that "the idea of Law and Order is essentially a bastard one". They add: "It is not properly included solely in the subject area of criminology and jurisprudence, or politics, because it is not really a subject or discipline at all. The most common sense in which the term is used is as a political slogan employed by conservative politicians to play on the fears of voters and thereby (hopefully) to secure election or re-election. . . . It encompasses the main issues and problems to which politicians refer when campaigning on a Law and Order programme: e.g., violent crime, police powers, demonstrations, drugs, pornography and punishment." This description has a familiar ring.

One writer says: "In one sense, order means regular array, condition in which every part of unit is in its right place, tidiness, normal or healthy or efficient state. In the broader meaning it denotes a prevalence of constituted authority, a law-abiding state, the absence of turbulence, riot and violent crime."[2] Apart from the fact that this description of order seemingly implies more a statement of faith than an assertion of fact, it is still useful as a working definition. The crucial question is: how is this type of order achieved?

At this point we come face to face with what our modern complex society has evolved, namely, a double system of social control which is concerned with the maintenance of an orderly and stable environment and "arises, in a sense, from a permanent, running compromise between constraint and freedom, between the interest of the individual and the goals of society."[3] Inherent in this system are those mechanisms and techniques used or developed by society to regulate the behaviour of persons to meet society's goals and needs or "to maintain itself as a coherent and

---

[1] Paul Ward and Greg Woods, *Law and Order in Australia* (Sydney: Angus and Robertson Pty Ltd, 1972), p. 1.

[2] *Law and Order in Canadian Democracy* (Ottawa: Edmond Cloutier, 1949), p. 9.

[3] Elaine Cumming, *Systems of Social Regulation* (New York: Atherton Press, 1968), p. 4.

functioning unity".[4] Their nature is extremely complex in even the simplest of societies.

On the one hand we have the informal social control system where "the people who constitute society make moral evaluations of all others around them on the basis of whatever moral code they hold valid".[5] The form of social control—as Homans demonstrated—"is the property of states of social relations, not something imposed from the outside".[6] The level of control, be it high or low, is determined by the kinds of social relationship that exist among the individuals who make up society, and their effectiveness in getting people to follow prescribed patterns of behaviour. This control is maintained by the rewards and punishments which are built into every relationship, and which are evident in the conferring and witholding of esteem, the sanctions of gossip, and the institutional, economic and moral pressures that underlie behaviour. "It is assumed that although everyone learns to submit to the control of others, there remain, even among the most conforming, fleeting tendencies toward unpredictable behaviour or unacceptable behaviour that arise from ignorance, error, incomplete learning of the rules, or circumstances beyond human contol."[7]

On the other hand, we have the formal social control system instituted by the body politic and its agencies and which is built on law. This legal-rational system for the regulation of human behaviour spells out relationships among people in terms of legal obligations and expectations and is a relatively late development in the history of the human race. Its main justification is that informal social control alone cannot maintain order in societies complicated enough for groups to have conflicting goals. "While the folkways and mores tend to achieve conformity in behaviour

[4] "The Rule of Law," *A Report to the National Commission on the Causes and Prevention of Violence* (Nashville: Aurora Publishers Inc., 1970), p. 36.

[5] Victor G. Stretchen, *The Environment of Law Enforcement* (Englewood Cliffs, N.J.: Prentice Hall, Inc., 1971).

[6] Michael Banton, *The Policeman in the Community* (London: Tavistock Publications, 1964), p. 4.

[7] E. Cumming, op. cit., p. 4.

by virtue of public opinion, group distaste of repugnance, ridicule and anger, they nonetheless usually have an optional character, particularly in modern complex societies, where wide variations in customary behaviour exist. The law, however, is meant to be applicable to all segments of the society and to impose the same degree of sanction, regardless of group, class, ethnic, and sectional differences."[8]

New Zealand, like all complex societies, has a profusion of governmental agencies, including the police, charged with the social control of individuals and which collectively make up the "bureaucracy". The bureaucracy—as Max Weber noted—"carries 'country action' into rationally ordered 'societal action'."[9] This is in fact what the State Departments and other public agencies do through the instrumentality of countless laws and regulations and under the auspices of government whose very *raison d'etre* for acceptance is, according to Milne,[10] "Protective, the maintenance of law and order".

In effect then, each governmental agency is a "law enforcer", and thus a formal agent of social control in its own right. It does, can only do, and make others do what the law directs or allows. Here we see the operation of the "rule of law", which (among other things) "expresses the idea that people recognise the legitimacy of the law as a means of ordering and controlling the behaviour of all the people in a society".[11] The law implies rational restraint upon the rules and procedures utilised to achieve order.

Nor is all this law of the "policy" or "administrative" variety. Much of it is criminal law, of which the police do not have a monopoly. Others, with their investigatory and/or regulatory power, who are not usually thought of as part of the police system are involved in enforcing it, such as Customs, Immigration, Indus-

---

[8] H. A. Bloch and G. Geis, *Man, Crime and Society* (New York: Random House, 1962), p. 37.

[9] N. J. Powell, *Responsible Public Bureaucracy in the United States* (Boston: Allyn and Bacon, Inc., 1967), p. 6.

[10] R. S. Milne, "The Inevitability of Administrative Discretion", *N.Z.J.P.A.*, 1967, p. 11.

[11] *Rule of Law,* op. cit., p. 8.

tries and Commerce, Traffic, Stock, Fishing, Post Office, Safety (Department of Labour) and Inland Revenue Inspectors and numerous others. This explains why only 21 percent of all offences taken to the criminal courts are handled by the police. An American professor[12] of sociology claims that it is even probable that the less visible offences with which the non-police agencies are concerned, as part of their work, are economically and even in terms of personal suffering, more costly to the community, than are the more visible offences dealt with by the police. This is a debatable question.

Yet the common fallacy—recently re-echoed by the Ombudsman[13] that the "task of law enforcement lies in the hands of the police", still remains and ignores the existence of numerous other public bodies who exercise formal social control by enforcing the law. More especially it tends to ignore that the "aim of preventing crime and thus maintaining order is shared by others in the correctional process—the probation officer, the social welfare officer, the Courts and the prison officer—all of whom are enforcing the law. All pursue this goal. "The difference is not one of objectives or aims, the difference is in the manner in which our specific roles contribute to the common goal of protecting society."[14]

Misner, in examining the American police functions, excluded "law enforcement" from his list and wrote: "This exclusion was conscious, for it appears that 'law enforcement' is epistemologically and logically a process and a consequence involving congeries of public agencies, including regulatory commissions, Courts, prosecutors, etc. Hopefully, some future paper will examine the rather curious use which is made of the term 'law enforcement' today."[15]

---

[12] A. Morris, "Correctional Research" (Massachusetts Correctional Association, 1969), p. 4.

[13] Sir Guy Powles, "The Ombudsman and the Law" *The N.Z. Justices Quarterly* (Vol. 41, No. 3), September 1972, p. 65.

[14] J. Braithwaite, "The Police in Corrections—Partnership or Conflict", *Police* (January-February 1967), p. 6.

[15] G. E. Misner, "The Urban Police Mission", *Issues in Criminology* (Vol. 3, No. 1, 1967), p. 35.

In New Zealand, it is no more accurate to refer to policemen in the uniform branch as "law enforcement officers" than it is to apply the term to magistrates, judges, probation officers, and lawyers. Using the term to describe policemen or their work carries long-term disadvantages as well. "It not only influences the individual policeman's definition of his job but also affects his priorities while on his job. . . . Organisationally, it . . . describes in advance the system of rewards . . . masks the fact that enforcement duties comprise a minor part of the typical policeman's daily routine."[16]

So far I have shown that two systems of social control—the moral evaluation process (informal) and the rationalised legal-institution (formal)—co-exist. The police are a part only of the latter system. On reflection it is self-evident that democratic society depends upon these systems for its survival, by and through which the behaviour of most of the population is made predictable most of the time.

We can now ask: which of these systems has the greatest impact in maintaining social control—in the sense of maintaining law and order? Banton answers this question by considering some of the variations in criminality. He looked at an average United States city of 500,000 people in which, in 1962, there were 36 cases of murder, 60 of rape, whereas in Edinburgh in the same year there were four murders and eight cases of rape. He reasoned that the Edinburgh figures are lower not because the police are more efficient but because the community is more orderly, i.e. it has a higher degree of informal social control. He concluded: "Law and law-enforcement agencies, important though they are, appear puny compared with the extensiveness and intricacy of these other modes of regulating behaviour. . . ."[17]

Banton's findings are supported by Derbyshire. He sums up the situation in this way: "Social control systems operate most effectively and efficiently, the police notwithstanding, where there is constant and unified, both overt and covert, cultural and social

---

[16] G. E. Misner, "Enforcement: Illusion of Security", *The Nation*, April 1969, p. 488.

[17] Banton, op. cit., p. 2.

support from all social control agencies. This support must be unambiguously stated in the value systems of families, community, and the greater society of which the individual is a functional part."[18]

Commenting generally on the effectiveness of the law as a regulator of human conduct, McIver noted: "The law remains a vast structural frame which cannot do more than limit the myriad relationships of men . . . the law, is too general, too clumsy, too formal, to touch the essentials of conduct. . . The state cannot possibly fulfil the purpose of the family or the church or the trade union or the cultural organisations. Not only because of its universality but still more because of its coercive sanction, the law of the state has a limited competence. The root of obedience to law is not coercive sanction but the will to obey: nevertheless law takes the form of an imperative. It can therefore regulate only the external order of society. Its unbending rigour is applicable only to the outer aspects of conduct."[19]

To the extent that it is true that: (a) no amount of police in a democratic society can replace the intricate, almost unconscious, network of voluntary controls and standards among the people themselves; and (b) the police are only one among many agencies of social control, I contend that the undoubted tendency for the police themselves and the larger community to over-identify police with the responsibility for maintaining law and order is not only illogical but it also has pernicious consequences. Let us look at some of these.

Immediately following an outbreak of crime, disorder, delinquency, vandalism, or other forms of anti-social behaviour, the public tends to look automatically to the police for the solution. Frequently they will demand publicly more police, or greater police activity. Politicians are inclined to respond by a promise of more police and more equipment. The underlying inference is that police will provide the answer. This can have the effect of

---

[18] R. L. Derbyshire, "The Social Control Role of the Police in Changing Urban Communities", *Exerpta Criminoligica* (Vol. 6, No. 3, 1966), p. 316.
[19] R. M. McIver, *The Modern State* (Oxford University Press, 1926), pp. 19-21.

diverting public attention from seeking more basic and long-term solutions.

Seldom is there any public discussion, not to mention research, concerning:

—discovery of, and removal of conditions, which might breed crime and disorder;

—the role of the community in the establishment and the enforcement of norms of conduct and the need for more effective mechanisms of informal social control;

—the social influence of the news media in general, and television in particular, in generating crime;

—the adequacy or otherwise of the socialisation process in homes and educational institutions in character formation;

—the responsibilities of religious institutions, professional organisations, social welfare workers, Courts, probation officers, trade unions, health authorities, civic groups, and the larger community in preventing crime and disorder.

This comment made by an American writer has a high degree of "local" application: "For too long our society has sought the solution for its crime problem exclusively in the area of improving and expanding its police services. Certainly we should seek constantly to improve our police services: it does seem to me that in expanding indefinitely our police forces we shall serve no useful purpose. The law of diminishing returns will come into play; the point of no further returns will soon be reached. . . ."[20]

It is of interest to witness in New Zealand the complete absence of community pressure groups to promote aid for victims of crime or a greater public understanding and awareness of problems relating to crime and disorder in the community. One notes too the inability of the Report of the Social and Cultural Committee to the National Development Conference (1969) to make any direct reference to crime and disorder, despite its mandate

---

[20] V. L. Broderick, "The Supreme Court and the Police: A Police Viewpoint", *The Journal of Criminal Law, Criminology & Police Science* Vol. 57, No. 3, 1966, p. 271.

to deal primarily with the "quality of life" and the attainment of a desirable social environment. Obviously the amount of crime and disorder in a community affects the quality of life.

In particular there is no public discussion or obvious public awareness of the difficulties which police have in mechanically preventing crime. Apart from the fact that a western-type democracy severely restricts police methods, the traditional emphasis placed on the power and ability of the police to prevent crime by mechanical means is an over-stated myth. The concept of mechanical prevention of crime assumes that the police will be physically present (or soon will be) where and at the time offences are intended to be committed. This combination of circumstances is a rarity. Even allowing for an inordinate increase in police numerical strength, police can only cover, geographically speaking, a fraction of a city or rural area at a particular time. With increasing urban sprawl, this inability is becoming more acute. What is more, the time, place and circumstances of crime cannot be predicted with any certainty. Prevention of crime through police action is based largely upon the projection of the threat of detection. However, once a mobile patrol (or beat constable) passes a particular spot, the probability of its or another's appearance is so slim and the speed at which a crime is committed generally is so great that the perpetrator's apprehension "risk" is quite low.

There are additional restraints which preclude mechanical crime prevention by police. It must be stressed that the "street crime" to which police might, in ideal circumstances, have access makes up only an infinitesimal portion of the total crime committed. Successful crime after all, is secret crime. The bulk of this is committed on private premises to which police do not have normal access. Neither can police reach those crimes which take place in family contexts or between acquaintances.

Moreover, much crime is of a type which is committed on impulse without regard for the presence of the police or other consequences. In any case, crime which is carefully premeditated is likely to be committed in a manner that militates against physical prevention by police.

"There are some crimes so irrational, so unpredictable, so explosive, so resistant to analysis or explanation that they can no more be prevented or guarded against than earthquakes or tidal waves."[21]

Much of the argument stressing the difficulties of the police in mechanically preventing crime applies also to the detection of crime. A few further points need to be made. Obviously, people who commit crimes do not leave their names and addresses at the crime scene. Nor does the modern criminal leave many other clues. Yet the public expects the police somehow to trace the persons who are responsible—preferably on the basis that the public itself does not become involved. The social custom is to avoid becoming involved, for the problem is viewed as purely a police one. "Informers" tend to be socially ostracised and the education system does little or nothing to remedy this. Once the police trace those whom they consider to be the perpetrators, they must observe all the ethical and legal niceties, even when the facts are confused, distorted, and the people involved are over-emotional or even temporarily insane.

Invariably, because of the absence of witnesses, or more frequently, their reluctance to become involved and face the uncomfortable and "accusing" atmosphere of the courts where they are frequently subjected to distress through severe cross-examination by defence lawyers, police are often forced into a position where they must rely on whatever admissions are made voluntarily by suspects as the main evidential base. Otherwise, in the majority of cases there is no evidence of sufficient strength to take the cases to Court. Indeed if all suspects were strictly to follow the directions of most solicitors, namely, not to admit anything to the police (this being the usual advice as all policemen know), instead of the offence detection rate in New Zealand being now about 50 percent, it could well finish up at about 10 percent. Is this what the community wants? The extent to which solicitors—in fulfilling their duty to clients—now con-

---

[21] *The Challenge of Crime in a Free Society*—A Report by the President's Commission on Law Enforcement and Administraation of Justice (U.S. Government Printer, 1967), p. 17.

tribute towards the unsolved crime rate in New Zealand would provide an interesting study.

It cannot realistically be expected that the police will be effective in detecting more than the few strongly and almost universally condemned and physically visible acts against which the public sense of outrage is the effective deterrent for most people. Perhaps it is time for New Zealand police and laymen to reflect on Wilson's statement: "But in crime prevention not too much should be expected of the police. I doubt that any deployment, any strategy, or any organizational principle will permit the police to make more than a slight or temporary reduction in the rate of most crimes. As the police themselves are fond of saying, 'we don't cause crime,' and, as I would like to see them add, 'we can't stop crime.' They can and should make arrests and they can and should investigate suspicious circumstances. . . . They can make no more than marginal gains, however they behave. It would be well, therefore, not to 'over-see' proposed improvements in police manpower . . . equipment or tactics. Already too many citizens share the dangerous view that if only we 'unleashed' the police we could stop crime dangerous because if we act on that assumption we are likely to produce only frustrated expectations and deeper passions."[22]

Much of what has been said so far is borne out by a survey recently carried out by Wilson among a representative sample of citizens in Melbourne, Sydney and Brisbane, as well as Laidley (a small rural township). Multi-phase random sampling procedures were used to select 1,018 people within each of the three metropolitan areas, and the rural area, to answer the question: "What do you think would be the most important thing that can be done here to cut down the amount of crime?" Respondents were given nine answers from which to make their selection, viz., heavier penalties; more police patrols and better methods; more youth clubs; better home environment; re-educate public on law (public relations through media); nothing can be done; change on an individual level; other; and don't know.

[22] James O. Wilson, "Dilemmas of Police Administration", *Public Administration Review* (September-October 1968), p. 415.

Wilson's survey findings and conclusions merit quoting in full:

". . . The sample thought the most important thing to be done to cut down on the amount of crime was to improve police efficiency either through providing more police, having more police patrols, or improving police efficiency by the police employing 'better methods.' With fifty-one per cent of the urban sample and fifty-five per cent of the rural sample suggesting this as the most important measure to cut crime, it is clear that the community sees the police as being not only the first but also the most important weapon to be used against crime. Heavier penalties, the second most referred to measure, was given by only twelve per cent of the sample. People, then, see crime as a police matter and, at least from the comments we recorded from those interviews, the public blame increased crime on lack of police efficiency or manpower.

"Few respondents thought the crime rate could be cut at the grass roots level. Thus reference to adverse economic and social conditions—explanations of criminality frequently given by social scientists—were rarely mentioned.

The vast majority of those interviewed did not consider better home environment, more youth clubs or more counselling services as being the main way to cut down crime. The public likens crime, then, as they liken so many other social problems, to a cancer; to most citizens the image of society and its problems is that of an essentially healthy organism invaded by alien substances. The police, in terms of crime and criminals, are seen as similar to physicians whose job it is to remove the cyst, destroy the virus, but without altering the character of the community itself. Unfortunately . . . such an analogy of crime and social problems seriously distorts social reality. As a professional criminologist . . . I do . . . know, however, that increasing police strength without making fundamental social and economic changes in society will do little to reduce the crime rate. Crime is interwoven with almost every aspect of Australian life and controlling it involves improving the quality of family life, the way schools are run, the way cities are planned and the way workers are hired. Controlling crime is not carried out only by using policemen as legislative surgeons. Controlling crime is rather the business of every Australian institution and, indeed, of every Australian . . . I am concerned with the tendency of both the public and politicians alike to leave crime control in the hands of the police. To most people crime prevention means no more than taking stop gap measures such as locking up houses and taking taxis at night. Facile and rather superficial proposals for curing crime such as employing more police do little to prevent crime. Crime control must be approached by every institution in Australia working in unison to solve an aspect of Australian life that directly or indirectly affects every individual in the community."[23]

It is reasonable to assume that Wilson's findings would reflect in large measure, the New Zealand attitude towards crime control.

If the general public believe, as they are inclined to do, that the police are the principal or only antidote to crime, this not only weakens society's sense of civic responsibility, but it also puts social pressure on the police to:

(a) " 'produce'—to be efficient rather than legal when the two norms are in conflict";[24]

(b) show a high "clearance" rate in order to maintain a "public image of themselves as productive in a market oriented society";[25] and

(c) settle things outside the courts to ensure that 'justice' is done.

How are police to resolve this conflict seeing that their self-concept is largely rooted in community expectations? Courts and lawyers are not slow, and rightly so, in criticising policemen who fail to develop cases that meet court standards. They do not appear to know or appreciate the community social pressures which can force policemen to "produce at all costs".

---

[23] Paul R. Wilson, "Crime and the Public", *Australian and N.Z. Journal of Criminology* (December 1971), pp. 231-232.

[24] Jerome H. Skolnick, *Justice Without Trial* (University of California, John Wiley & Sons, Inc., 1966), p. 231.

[25] Albert J. Reiss (Jr.) and David J. Burdea, "Environment and Organisation: A perspective on the Police' in Bordua (ed.), *The Police: Six Sociological Essays,* (New York: John Wiley & Sons, Inc., 1967), p. 33.

When one looks at the New Zealand scene and notes the press statements, the well-publicised comments of some politicians and the conversational comments one hears from members of the public in relation to demonstrators and other groups who act "differently" there is ample evidence to suggest that the larger conservative community often expects the police to rid cities of undesirable persons, and keep the unsightly off the streets even though the police do not have the legal means of doing so. Policemen learn how hypocritical the public can be and how difficult it is to effectively mediate between cries for police intervention in these situations and the hostility which such intervention evokes. It is not, and should not be part of the police role to act as a "community bully". There is always the danger that some policemen caught between these demands and those of the law that circumscribe the methods by which they may exert social control, could unconsciously tend to identify themselves with the larger and more conservative community and its social pressures.

To do so, however, might ease middle-class anxiety, but it would accomplish little in dealing with the underlying causes of anti-social behaviour. It is to this premise that many observers of the police fail to look. "Our communities very often seem to want their police 'to make people good'—a commendable goal, but not the proper function of police. Our communities often seem to want their police to protect the community from 'the questioner of the status quo', the non-conformist, and such a desire, in these days of social protest, is unrealistic. Our extremists are questioning moderation, our peace demonstrators are questioning militarism, our minorities are questioning racism, our hippies are questioning materialism, and our youth are questioning the hypocrisy of their elders; and no police agency of integrity can allow itself to be misused as an instrument for the harassment of unpopular ideas."[26]

Goldstein, a noted writer on American police affairs, remarked:

[26] A. C. Germann, "Community Policing: An Assessment", *The Journal of Criminal Law, Criminology and Police Science* (Vol. 60, No. 1, 1969), p. 90.

"Most law enforcement officials long ago resigned themselves to the role of the underdog upon whom the unsolved problems of society were piled high. Having developed what might best be termed a defensive posture, the police have, for example, widely accepted responsibility for all that is criminal despite the fact that crimes are not committed by the police, but rather by the citizens of the communty they serve. How often do we hear a police official admonish a community for a rise in crime? How often does a police official point an accusing finger at conditions which produce crime and criminals? Instead whenever the publication of crime statistics indicates a rise in crime, he feels that he has in some way failed and that his department has failed. In carrying such a burden, the average police official sees nothing especially strange about having to carry a responsibility for a type of enforcement he is unable to fulfil. He has learned two characteristics of his job: he must bear this burden well and he must refrain from discussing it lest it be a source of embarrassment to him and his community."[27]

What then is the answer? Do the police have *the* responsibility for maintaining law and order? A Commission set up in 1967 by the Board of Social Responsibility in England reached this conclusion after two years' work: "The prevention of crime, the detection and punishment of offenders, the protection of life and property and the preservation of public tranquility must be the objectives of the public themselves—both in general and in detail —and must be the direct responsibilities of ordinary citizens who are organized for the purpose. In this the police are given certain functions and duties to enable the public to do its work. The achievement of Sir Richard Mayne's objectives [shown in the first sentence of this quotation] cannot simply be left to the police. It is destructive both of police and of public social health to attempt to pass over to the police the obligations and duties associated with the prevention of crime and the preservation of public tranquility. These are obligations and duties of the public aided *by the police and not the police aided by the public. This*

---

[27] H. Goldstein, "Police Discretion: The Ideal versus the Real", *Public Administrative Review* (September 1963), p. 140.

emphasis is crucial and much of the uneasiness about police and community relationships stems from getting the emphasis wrong. It is necessary to place the duty of maintaining law and order on the community aided by the police, rather than on the police occasionally aided by public-spirited citizens."[28]

The initiative necessary to bring about this reorientation in both public and police thinking largely lies initially with the police themselves. It will be a long but necessary process. Annual reports to Parliament, press statements and police literature generally will need to reflect this new emphasis. Public training and educational institutions must play their part. I have yet to hear or read of a New Zealand police administrator publicly propounding that "the function of the police is to aid the public in maintaining law and order". Rather, the police tendency is publicly to state that "police are responsible for maintaining law and order"— followed invariably by admonition that the public do not co-operate enough to solve police problems. These are, of course, the community's problems; this point should and must be stressed.

This change of emphasis is more than a semantic distinction or play on words. ". . . We should remember that the grammar of any language is itself a shaper of ideas, the programme and guide for the individual's mental activity, for his analysis of impressions, for his synthesis of his mental stock and trade." [29] There is a significant difference between police saying "Our responsibility is to maintain law and order and we ask you (the public) to help" and saying "Our responsibility is to help you (the public) to maintain law and order". The essential difference is that an old myth is being replaced by a more credible one or at least one which, in short, is more useful, is closer to reality, is more democratic, places responsibility where it belongs, and engenders greater community interest in policing itself. The problem and

---

[28] *Police: A Social Study* (London: Church Army Press, 1967), p. 58.
[29] B. L. Whorf, "Science and Linguistics in John B. Carroll" (ed.), *Language Thought and Reality* (New York: Wiley and Technology Press, 1956), p. 212. Quoted by M. Landau, in "The Concept of Decision Making in the 'Field' of Public Administration", Mailick/Van Ness (ed.), *Concepts and Issues in Administrative Behaviour* (Prentice-Hall, Inc., 1962), p. 26.

duty of the administrator is to minimise the gap between myth and reality.

I see this change of emphasis having a practical and psychological significance in structuring the role and orientation of the community to maintain law and order. At the same time, it has a concomitant effect on how the police mission is carried out (e.g. helping the community to "police" themselves) and it is a recognition of the interdependence between all segments of the New Zealand community in the maintenance of law and order and in other phases of community development which contribute constructively to democratic living. The evidence might suggest that wherever irresponsibility or rebellion have threatened or interrupted the peace of the community, invariably it has been traceable to the shirking of duty by many elements in that community.

It is often argued by writers, with considerable over-stress in my view, that the police are the logical candidates for holding the key responsibility (on behalf of the government) for maintaining law and order, because they are the "first-line" of the coercive force of society. How realistic is this argument? In the first place it ignores the value of informal social control as a means towards helping to maintain law and order. But force, as Lindsay correctly observes is an ambiguous word. "If we mean by it pressure put by a person or persons on others in order to make them do what without such pressure they would not have done, such pressure is exercised by all sorts of persons and associations. . . ."[30]

But merely because police, in certain circumstances, have the power to arrest, to use physical force to prevent serious injury to persons or to prevent a breach of the peace—is this a sufficient argument for saying that the police are society's "first-line" possessors of coercive force? In practical terms, the community itself —as a recent Auckland survey[31] shows—reports a little less than 100 percent of all specific incidents handled by the police. To

---

[30] A. D. Lindsay, *The Modern Democratic State,* Volume 1 (Oxford University Press, London, 1943), p. 198.

[31] This survey will be discussed in the next chapter.

say the least, the community is the "trigger" for physical coercive force. Moreover, a study of the law clearly indicates that there are few circumstances in which police have physical coercive powers over and above that legally granted to each and every citizen. In addition, in every case where a policeman can initiate criminal proceedings, so too can private citizens by way of "private" prosecutions. If we equate the state with the community then it is correct to say that the community itself possesses the coercive powers.

Could it not be argued that social scientists and the legal fraternity have over-spent their energies in debating the coercive powers of the police instead of coming to grips with such issues as: the root causes of the social problems which manufacture "criminals" and anti-social conduct; why many youngsters are not provided with training to cope with the human demands of living in a consumer and largely materialistic society; why many youngsters feel alienated from the larger community, feel bereft of stable values and see much of the law as being repugnant; why the majority of witnesses dread having to appear in court to give evidence; why there are no civic groups to help the victims of crime; the role and responsibility of all segments of the community to maintain law and order. Coercive force comes into play especially when these issues are neglected.

Up to this point, we have tried to show that the community's tendency to over-identify the police with the responsibility for law and order is illogical, especially as the police are only one agency of social control. This tendency has and is resulting in a community failure to recognise the value of the informal social control system as a regulator of human conduct. Above all, this tendency is distracting the community from recognising its own responsibility for maintaining law and order.

In accepting the blanket responsibility to prevent and detect crime and to preserve order, police have in effect been trying to "go it alone". The number of reported offences and crimes rises remorselessly in spite of more police and better deployment and mobility of police staff. There can be many explanations for this trend. Somewhere the basic fact has been lost sight of: that the public not the police, controls the volume of crime.

Policemen as a whole must change the attitudes they have towards their role, and emphasise publicly that their responsibility is to *aid* the community in preventing and detecting crime, and in maintaining order. This change of emphasis is by no means an attempt to denigrate the preventive worth of the police. Rather it is a case of placing responsibility where it belongs. It is an open and necessary recognition that police ability to maintain an orderly and safe democratic society is limited. For too long police have dogmatised their own ability in this direction.

Exploration of these issues also brings into focus the polarisation of attitudes which has occurred concerning the role of the police, and the tendency of government and governmental agencies to avoid their own responsibilities in these matters and use the police as a scapegoat when social problems reach critical proportions. Alongside this has been public apathy and indifference, and the unfortunate public tendency to overdepend on, and use the police as a "scarecrow" device to solve social ills. Should these trends continue, it is likely that Parliament will gradually introduce a stream of restrictive legislative measures in the name of law and order—with the consequential effect of eroding democratic principles, and making the policeman's task even more difficult. What then? In a complex, urbanised democratic country it is simply not possible for police to shoulder a disproportionate responsibility for law and order and still operate by the rule of law.

3

Nature and Realities of Police Work: Its Social Content

The conception of the policeman's role is of major importance in defining the nature of police-community relations. The nature of such relationships is determined to a large extent by the way in which police see their functional role and also by the way in which others see it.

While each person has a somewhat different impression of the nature of the police role, based to some extent on his personal experiences and contacts (or the lack of them) with policemen, there is a widespread popular misconception of the police, supported by news and entertainment media. Through these, the police have come to be viewed largely as a body of men engaged in apprehending and prosecuting criminals. Emphasis upon this one dramatic aspect of police functioning has led to a tendency on the part of both the public and the police to underestimate the range and complexity of the total police task, and to ignore much of it or treat it as being of little importance.

Many policemen themselves, over the years, have been quite successful in reinforcing the "cops and robbers" conception by claiming that "enforcing the laws" is the primary objective of the New Zealand police. The police department's annual reports to Parliament, for example, place heavy emphasis on offences and crimes reported to the police. Police involvement in youth aid work, crime prevention, and search and rescue also feature but to a much lesser extent. For the most part, these reports do not do justice to the range and diversity of the duties that police undertake—many of which are as important as they are time-consuming, and as constructive as they are unproductive (in some cases) of paper records.

Before looking at the range of these duties, it may be useful to refer to recent studies conducted overseas. Various studies in America where police do, in fact, have a wider range of laws to enforce than their New Zealand counterparts, have shown that only a small percentage of police work involves actual law enforcement. Johnson and Gregory[1] summarise these studies: "Epstein estimated that 90 per cent of the policeman's function is in activities unrelated to crime control or law enforcement. Cumming, et al, reported that half of the calls for assistance to an urban police department may involve family crises or other complaints of a personal or inter-personal nature. Parnas, studying just one month of Chicago's 1966 police records, reported that of a total of 134,369 calls for police in the City of Chicago, 17 per cent were classified as 'Criminal Incident'. The remaining 83 per cent includes 12,544 traffic accident calls and 96,826 'Miscellaneous Non-Criminal'. This 'Miscellaneous Non-Criminal' category includes about 80 per cent of all calls for police service. Misner indicated that police departments have new missions in urban situations. The assumption has been that the policeman's task is to control crime and investigate criminals. Misner reports that more than 80 per cent of police time has been spent in non-criminal matters. These non-criminal, inter-personal incidents include anything from a cat caught in a tree to a family quarrel, to runaway children, to neighbours making too much noise. In other words, the policeman makes very few arrests in comparison to the 'human relations' work that he does."

Could such overseas findings also apply to New Zealand? What

[1] D. Johnson & R. T. Gregory, "Police Community Relations in the United States: A Review of Recent Literature and Projects", *Journal of Criminal Law, Criminology and Police Science* (Vol. 62, No. 1), 1971, pp. 95-96.

calls are made by the public on the New Zealand police and what are the nature of such cases? To answer these questions I probed the largest area of police field activity—the mobile patrol vehicles (both Uniform Branch and C.I.B.) in the Auckland Metropolitan District, which has a population of 767,000 and covers 2,352 land square miles. The survey ranged over a continuous three-week period, both day and night shifts, from 1 July 1972 to 21 July 1972, during which time all field "incidents" reported by the public and despatched to patrol vehicles were recorded as well as the police action taken in respect of each "incident". "On-view incidents" investigated by the police on their own initiative were similarly recorded.

During the survey period a total of 4,600 "incidents" were recorded. The functional aspects of these "incidents" were examined with a view to describing, along with statistical accounting, the reality of police work. As the following table indicates, they are grouped under eight categories labelled "Preventive", "Community Services", "Traffic", "Force on Person", "Property Damage", "General Misconduct", "Property Appropriation", and "Sexual Offences". "Community Services" is a convenient category which, in a different context, could aptly be applied to all incidents.

CLASSIFICATION OF 4,600 "INCIDENTS" ATTENDED BY AUCKLAND METROPOLITAN POLICE PATROL VEHICLES DURING CONTINUOUS THREE-WEEK PERIOD
(1.7.72 to 21.7.72)

PREVENTIVE (not including passive patrolling):

	Number of tasks	% of total
Road block	44	.96
Burglar alarm attended	198	4.30
Recover missing motor vehicles	71	1.54
Escape ex. institution	14	.30
Question loiterers	85	1.85
Insecure premises	85	1.85
Others	57	1.24
Total	554	12.04

COMMUNITY SERVICES:

	Number of tasks	% of total
Assist at fires	21	.46
Trace/advise relatives	171	3.72
Deaths (sudden, etc.)	79	1.72
Missing persons	125	2.72
Noisy parties/disturbances near dwellings	204	4.43
Disputes, family, etc.	444	9.65
Mental illness	34	.74
Other assistance to public (miscellaneous)	291	6.33
Total	1369	29.76

PROPERTY DAMAGE:

	Number of tasks	% of total
Damage	145	3.15
Arson	16	.34
Others	20	.43
Total	181	3.93

GENERAL MISCONDUCT:

	Number of tasks	% of total
Language, obscene, etc.	22	.48
Idle and disorderly	15	.33
Drunkenness	52	1.13
Liquor in public, at dance, etc.	3	.07
Fighting	143	3.11
Behaviour, disorderly, etc.	164	3.57
Gaming	6	.13
Trespass	74	1.61
Others	58	1.26
Total	537	11.67

TRAFFIC:

	Number of tasks	% of total
Traffic offence (not motor accident or intoxicated in charge	34	.74
Motor accidents with injury, etc.	262	5.70
Drunk in charge (or suspected)	46	1.00
Others	14	.30
Total	356	7.74

FORCE ON PERSON:

							Number of tasks	% of total
Assault	....	....	....	....	....	....	131	2.85
Robbery	....	....	....	....	....	....	29	.63
Neglect	....	....	....	....	....	....	9	.20
Homicide	....	....	....	....	....	....	17	.37
Others	....	....	....	....	....	....	9	.20
						Total	195	4.24

PROPERTY APPROPRIATION:

							Number of tasks	% of total
Credit by fraud	....	....	....	....	....		23	.50
Theft	....	....	....	....	....	....	540	11.74
"Taking", interfering with motor vehicle			....		....		199	4.33
False pretence	....	....	....	....		....	18	.39
Burglary	....	....	....	....	....	....	572	12.43
Others	....	....	....	....	....	....	14	.30
						Total	1366	29.70

SEXUAL OFFENCES:

							Number of tasks	% of total
Obscene exposure/indecent act, etc.				....		....	16	.35
Indecent assault	....	....	....	....	....		3	.07
Rape	....	....	....	....	....	....	2	.04
Others	....	....	....	....	....	....	21	.46
						Total	42	.91

A new perspective on police activity resulted from this analysis. Of the 4,600 "incidents" investigated by patrol personnel:

(a) "Preventive" together with "Community Service" incidents exceeded all other incidents (not including "Property Appropriation").

(b) "Preventive" together with "Community Service" incidents nearly exceeded all other incidents ("Traffic" excluded).

(c) Domestic disputes (intra-familial type) alone exceeded "Force on Person", "Property Damage" and "Sexual Offences" combined.

(d) The number of "Community Service" dispatches exceeded any other single category and constituted 29.76 percent of all incidents.

(e) Only 230 incidents (or 5 percent) resulted in arrests by patrol personnel which clearly shows that other alternatives are preferred to this exercise of formal social control.

(f) About 60 percent of all incidents were dealt with "on the spot" without any further police action.

(g) Ninety-seven percent of all incidents (including the "Preventive" category) were initially reported to the police by the public.

(h) There is no evidence to suggest that the type and range of activities undertaken by the Auckland police are significantly different to those undertaken by police in other large cities in New Zealand.

The core service provided by the Auckland police was one of service and protection. The decisions to protect were triggered almost entirely by the community itself. In other words, citizens reported incidents after they had occurred or asked for other varied forms of police assistance. That this is so confirms the theory discussed earlier that police cannot make any significant impact on preventing crime and offences by sheer mechanical means. For the most part, what police are doing is strategically positioning their patrols so that they can respond rapidly to citizens' requests for help. Hopefully, their mere presence and patrolling activities have some crime deterrent value, as well as providing citizens with a feeling of safety and security.

The main conclusion to be drawn from the Auckland survey is that the police are in fact spending a great deal of their effort on matters other than actual crime or conduct which is serious enough to call for arrest or prosecution. To view police activity solely from the standpoint of law enforcement is to miss the crux of the police role. It is considered that more than 70 percent of the total dispatches shown in the Auckland survey did not involve law enforcement as such.

These include: keeping the peace; protecting people from

potential violence; settling and mediating in family, landlord/ tenant disputes, quarrels and diverse forms of crises; aiding the sick, insane, emotionally disturbed and the potential suicide; dealing with sudden deaths, deaths from accidents and other misadventure; locating missing persons; returning lost children; counselling children; eliminating public nuisances and meeting a variety of public requests for support or assistance with problems of health, safety, injury, illness, or inter-personal relationships. This list does not include duties carried out by the non-patrolling police. For example, since 1958, the police youth section has dealt with 65,000 cases of troubled/troublesome or delinquent children who were not taken to Court. In 1971 police arranged, participated in and controlled 726 search and rescue operations in relation to citizens who met with or were suspected of having met with mishaps at sea, in the bush, or elsewhere.

By the way, it is an interesting phenomenon that there is no National Council for Civil Liberties or other pressure group to watch over the manner in which the police carry out the above duties. Not only has no Government, no Court, ever said that many of these things are to be done properly, but neither has any legislator said that they are to be done at all.

This array of duties indicates that frontline policemen are essentially peace officers or conflict resolvers, rather than law enforcement officers. They serve as one of the agencies that help in maintaining some community integration and order. Through their activities, they attempt to bring peace to personal disputes and to those that arise from conflicts of values and between various sections of the community.

These activities could be classified broadly under the headings of "protecting life" and "preserving the peace". Protection of life extends to all such acts as may generally be termed "offences against the person", to unwarrantable infringements of liberties; and it extends special protection to the more vulnerable or easily exploited groups—e.g., children, the mentally feeble and the incapacitated. The preservation of public peace is a many-sided activity. It may require the mere passive presence of police at a religious procession, open-air meeting, or more active measures to ensure reasonable order and to prevent violence during political demonstrations. The reasons for police involvement in non-criminal activities are seldom found in the formulae of statutes but in considerations that are related to established practices of dealing informally with community problems. This is especially so when the policeman mediates and acts as a conciliator in family problems and such like and which grow out of the mundane problems of living—finances, alcohol, infidelity, family discipline, and so on. Parties may accept his advice because he is a policeman and they see him as an impartial figure. He has no legal power to compel them to act as he advises, but as the holder of an office, they imagine that he has the necessary legal authority. Bittner says: "Although this work cannot be subsumed under the concept of legal action, it does involve the exercise of a form of authority that most people associate with the police. In fact no matter how trivial the occasion, the device of calling the police transforms any problem. It implies that the situation is, or is getting out of hand. Police responses to public demands are always orientated to this implication, and the risks of proliferation of troubles make every call a potentially serious matter."[2] By tradition, policemen are supposed to help people in trouble. This explains in part why there is hardly a human predicament imaginable for which police aid has not been solicited at one time or another.

It is not generally realised that there is no substantive offence of "breaching the peace", nor is such a breach susceptible to any cut and dried definition. Yet, according to the police regulations, the policeman is expected to prevent it. In today's social climate, Rolph's[3] description of a "breach of the peace", such as "cocking a snook at the village constable to crowning university steeples with homely earthenware", would hardly suffice. A breach of the peace implies a prior definition of "peace", and this is a matter on which persons commonly disagree. Bittner

[2] Egon Bittner, "The Police on Skid-Row: A study of peace keeping", *American Sociological Review* (Vol. 32, No. 5), October 1967, p. 703.
[3] C. H. Rolph, *Common Sense about Crime and Punishment* (London: Victor Gollancz LT1, 1961), p. 67.

suggests that "peace keeping appears to be an unknown problem arrived at by unknown means".[4]

In one sense, maintaining the peace always involves giving support to some members of the community. It can also mean controlling other members. The Auckland survey previously described showed that 97 percent of all police activities were public requests for support of some kind. Although few were directly related to actual enforcement of the law, all were however supportive of some aspect of the welfare of the community.

Aside from the fact that there is a community demand for police to deal with non-criminal activities, it is useful to advance a step further and ask: why do the police tend to act as all-purpose remedial agents? This question is relevant because in the past many policemen and laymen have considered that such activities are only marginally related to the police mandate. This view fails to reckon with the fact that the police assign a substantial amount of their resources to such work.

Cumming[5] *et al.,* after conducting intensive studies of police activities in a large American city explained why police are asked to respond to a variety of social problems: ". . . The policeman has to do much of what he does because he is on duty at times of the day when no other agent is available. . . . He deals with the problems of a group of people—the poor and the ignorant—that studies of our own and others have shown no other agent to be anxious to serve, and . . . he has . . . access to, very few other agents. In other words, he is part of an integrative system in which the labour is divided not so much on the basis of function as on the basis of the time of day and the nature of the target population. All citizens can count on emergency help from the police when there is sudden illness at night. . ."

This finding substantially applies to the New Zealand situation. Citizens seeking help after-hours in respect of the matters mentioned under the heading of "Community Services", especially

[4] Bittner, op. cit., p. 701.
[5] Elaine Cumming, *et al.* "Policeman as Philosopher, Guide and Friend", *Social Problems* (Vol. 12), Winter 1965, p. 286.

domestic disputes and all types of emergency situations have, in the main, no agent to turn to except the police. Sir Thaddeus McCarthy recently said: "I hold the view that a police officer's value extends beyond what might strictly be called the administration of justice, certainly far beyond the pursuit of criminals. I accept Norval Morris's view that of all social workers in the community the police officer is perhaps the most important."[6]

A social study conducted by a Commission of eminent churchmen and policemen constituted by the Church Assembly Board in England in 1967 makes this point: "However representative he is of the law, and however much his presence in the community stands upon law, his normal encounter with most people, most of the time, is not in terms of law, nor is it to do, directly, with the law; it is in terms of a service to the community for which his uniform is his warrant; it guarantees, in the public eye, a standard of competence and a readiness to help which the public have now come to expect. If indeed, they now 'take it for granted' a little too readily, this is an indirect tribute to the men, who, by their service, have created the expectation."[7]

There is now a considerable volume of overseas opinion all pointing to a recognition that police work is in fact social work. In any case, how can crimes be described as anything other than a social problem? Even if the view is taken that mechanically preventing and detecting crime is not social work, the Auckland survey showed that the bulk of work undertaken by the uniformed police had a considerable social content. In addition, I cannot agree with those sociologists who describe the criminal catching and related activities of the police as being "law enforcement" and other activities as "Social Welfare". Why the distinction? Clearly, law enforcement is an adjunct to social control. As such, it is one of the functions conducive to the general social welfare by helping to secure the social order.

---

[6] The Rt. Hon. Sir Thaddeus McCarthy, "The Role of the Police in the Administration of Justice" in Clark, ed., *Essays on Criminal Law in New Zealand* (Wellington: Sweet & Maxwell (N.Z.) Ltd., 1971), pp. 174-175.
[7] *Police: A Social Study,* published for the Church Assembly Board for Social Responsibility (London: Church Army Press, 1967), p. 10-11).

It is unfortunate that the social work carried out by police is not fully recognised by other social work agents in New Zealand. It would seem that many of these agents, intent on maintaining their presumed monopoly on human relations, prefer to view police work as "authority-orientated", and therefore devoid of a social welfare content.

The fact that police, social workers, probation officers, community or local authority welfare officers operate to a large extent in relative isolation without any formal co-ordinating machinery, would seem a waste of useful knowledge and expertise and an undoubted display of collective shortsightedness in coming to grips with community welfare problems. Here, one can detect what appears to be a failure of integration within the system. Probably Robson had this problem in mind when he wrote, "Each province should fulfil its purpose adequately and is entitled to expect the other provinces to fulfil theirs. Those in one province should also have a broad yet clear understanding of what takes place in the others if only because what is done in one very often has an impact on the other provinces. In addition, there is need for co-ordination and especially in the realm of research. All this can occur without detriment to integrity, existing conventions and good practice."[8]

Hopefully in a more enlightened climate somewhere in the distant future all governmental social workers (including the police) and probation officers will unite and operate together as a closely-knit team with a common aim to prevent and to deal with the results of social problems. In 1968, the Commissioner of Police of the metropolis of London wrote: ". . . I am convinced that for too long there has been a gap between those services [social welfare] and the police and that, for the common good, an attempt should be made to fill the void . . . [police] possess an unequalled fund of local knowledge—of persons, their families and associates and of the atmosphere and philosophy which surrounds them. Assessments are mature and based upon

[8] J. L. Robson, "Crime and Penal Policy", *N.Z.J.P.A.* (Vol. 33, No. 2), March 1971, p. 50.

factual knowledge. If reforms are to work, I am convinced that the police must be accepted in a much fuller role."[9]

That there is a "wall", albeit eroding, between some of the professional social workers and some policemen is apparent. Both sides tend to see each other as stereotypes, and stereotypes feed largely on ignorance. Often these stereotypes are reinforced by fleeting experiences and over-hasty judgments. To the police-trained mind with its emphasis on order, organisation and discipline, the lack of system and commitment to rules and paper (probably only a lesser commitment) operating in a more discursive atmosphere associated with the social worker, adds substance to the stereotype.

Etzioni[10] is attempting to explain the uneasy interaction between police and social welfare agencies when he says: "In part, their relations are determined by ecological factors—for instance, by the degree to which the police and the welfare agencies concentrate in the same area. The larger the ecological contact, the higher the need for patterning the interaction. The general cultural 'tone' is another important factor. . . . In general, especially over recent decades, the public has tended to accept more and more the philosophy held by social welfare agencies [regarding treatment of offenders] . . . and less the traditional police approach [believed to be a punitive one]. In cases of conflict, the press, public, and to a degree the politicians tend to side with the welfare agencies, a fact which affects the relationship between the two organisations."

All welfare organisations, including the police, could usefully adopt Kramer's[11] argument for effective teamwork which, he stated, must begin with recognition and acceptance of the following six principles which might constitute a creed:

(a) We are all members of a single, inclusive profession of

---

9 Sir Joseph Simpson, "The Police and Juvenile Delinquency", *The British Journal of Criminology,* Vol 8, 1968, pp. 127-129.
10 A. Etzioni, *Modern Organisations* (New Jersey: Prentice Hall, 1964), p. 112.
11 Ralph M. Kramer, "Dynamics of Teamwork in the Agency, Community and Neighbour", *Social Work* (Vol. 1, No. 3), July 1956, pp. 56-57.

social work united by a common philosophy and objective —to help people attain satisfactory personal and social goals.

(b) We are all concerned with the same human needs and problems.

(c) We all share a common body of specialised knowledge which is applicable to these problems.

(d) We all have a common core of basic professional methods, skills, and processes which are applicable in our dealings with individuals, groups, and communities.

(e) We all share certain fundamental concepts such as the right of self-determination of individuals and groups; the importance of a non-judgmental attitude; the recognition of causal factors in behaviour, and the confidential nature of any material exchanged dealing with our work.

(f) We are on common ground in that we serve the same community and the people in it, and therefore we can make a more significant contribution if we work together than if we work independently.

The increasing burden of public demands on the police in recent years has resulted in policemen themselves questioning how far they should be involved in dealing with matters that seem to bear no direct relationship to the routine work of crime prevention and detection and preserving public order. The scope of this paper does not allow a detailed examination of what is or what is not a legitimate police function. However, general comments will be made.

As an opening, it might be useful to reflect on Goldstein's[12] comment which helps to neutralise what might appear to be unkind words directed earlier at the social welfare agencies:

"Behind much of the desire to rid the police of tasks unrelated to crime has been the reluctance of the police to become involved in anything closely identified with social work or social workers. Except for their contacts with juveniles, the police have tried hard to avoid engaging in programmes that commit them to

[12] H. Goldstein, "Police Response to Urban Crisis", *Public Administration Review*, September-October 1968, p. 419.

working with individuals and their problems on a continuing basis.

"They have strongly resisted occasional pressures to deal with chronic alcoholics, prostitutes, and narcotics addicts as other than criminal offenders. Within the juvenile field, in which social work techniques have now been employed for many years, officers assigned to working with juveniles still find themselves in a somewhat hostile departmental environment. Traditionally, police hope to be feared by prospective law violators. They view social workers as having quite different value systems, with a permissive attitude that is inconsistent with efforts at control."

Goldstein's comment is over-exaggerated in the New Zealand context, but it still has a ring of truth. Even so, New Zealand policemen cannot be blamed for wishing to avoid becoming heavily involved in basic social reform. Apart from the unrealistic demands made upon them to "cure" crime problems, they operate in a society which seems to believe that sanctions effectively administered will deter the evil-doer. The community persistence of this doctrinaire view concerning deterrence understandably forces the policeman to see his role in terms of crime repression only.

It is doubtful whether a firm and long-lasting decision can be made as to what in fact are legitimate police functions. Objectives must change from time to time to meet new demands and a changing environment. Obviously, police will always be involved in helping the community to feel secure both in person and property. There will be many peripheral duties in which there will be a doubt as to whether they rightly belong to the police. Perhaps the question to ask is whether those peripheral duties reduce or enhance police ability to carry out effectively their statutory duties of helping the community to protect life and property and to preserve public peace? This question is particularly relevant.

It must be remembered that the success of the police in a democracy is vitally dependent on public support and good-will. If the public withdraw their support or provide only token support then the police cannot help but be less effective servants. Therefore it can be argued that police should not be carrying out certain negatively loaded duties (e.g. collecting fines and serving summonses on behalf of the Justice Department), which lessen their ability to help in protecting the public, do not enhance their public image, and which do not need: "(a) the special qualifications and personal qualities demanded on entry to the police service; (b) the particular training provided within the police.[13] However, in recent years the police department has been gradually divesting itself of such duties. Chappell and Wilson take the view that "many of the tasks which police are asked to perform do hinder their major function of preventing and detecting crime." They add: ". . . police duties and responsibilities will certainly become much more complex, and the need has become pressing to determine the nature of the role to be played by police in the latter half of the twentieth century."[14]

It must be remembered that services such as youth aid work, giving advice to the community on how to prevent crime and protect itself from criminal activities, search and rescue activities, attending intra-familial problems are important in the total perspective of the police role. Performance of these services publicly show the police in the more positive role as "protectors" rather than "punitive agents". Undoubtedly the protective image facilitates community co-operation in dealing with the difficult aspects of crime control. "Often, it is these essentially secondary duties which give to the policeman, the public acceptance and co-operation which assists him in accomplishing what he considers to be his primary duties."[15]

Some further justification for positive but peripheral police work must be found, other than the fact that such work induces public co-operation in dealing with menacing forms of crime. This justification is exemplified by writers in this way: "Patrolmen should be practical social workers and encourage persons to come to them for assistance and advice when in trouble.

[13] *Police Manpower, Equipment and Efficiency: Reports of Three Working Parties* (H.M.S.O. London, 1967), pp. 28-29.
[14] D. Chappell and P. R. Wilson, *The Police and the Public in Australian and New Zealand* (University of Queensland Press, 1969), p. 171.
[15] G. E. Misner, op. cit., p. 38.

Distress situations are frequently symptoms of deep-rooted social ills that, if not corrected, may result in criminal or other anti-social behaviour which adversely affects the remainder of the life of the individual. By giving assistance, advice, and sympathy to those in distress, patrolmen help prevent wasted lives and also win friendship and co-operation for the department."[16]

". . . What the police require is an area of action which will facilitiate their being identified in a helpful role rather than a punitive role."[17]

"Crime prevention is not limited to positive police activity. Anything that contributes to the community's well-being adds to the preservation and protection of the peace within it. There-fore, it may become a cause for positive police action. Of course, no police department can be everywhere, trying to fulfil every community need. However, an efficient police should be con-tinually on the lookout for ways to contribute to the com-munity's peace and harmony."[18]

This chapter has shown in particular that the citizen's demands or expectations of police service are not confined to services con-cerning criminal activity. In fact the New Zealand police perform a varied and heavy assortment of social welfare functions. This mixture can create role strains—stemming from the difficulties of being caught in a crossfire of competing claims. It can also cause young policemen to doubt the legitimacy of those duties which do not appear to be directly related to crime and disorder control. But there will be less doubt if such duties are recognised and valued by all police leaders and the community alike as being part and parcel of the police role.

[16] Quoted from O. Wilson, *Police Administration,* in R. I. Parnas, "Police Response to the Domestic Disturbance", *Wisconsin Law Review* (Vol. 1967:914), p. 956.

[17] T. A. Johnson, "Police-Citizen Encounters and the Importance of Role Conceptualization for Police Community Relations" *Issues in Crimin-ology* (Vol. 7, No. 1), Winter 1972, p. 109.

[18] G. E. Berkley, *The Democratic Policeman* (Boston: Beacon Press, 1969), p. 205.

4

Police Discretion: Its Use, Validity, Source and Control

Much police work in our democracy requires considerable discretionary judgment before deciding what action is appropriate. Police discretion is a contentious subject but the way in which it is exercised "will very much determine the nature of the police role"[1] and the quality of police/public relations. ". . . Discretion is not something that can be considered apart from . . . the policeman's role in society."[2]

Police discretion is usually discussed in terms of police committal to the concept of "full enforcement" of laws or something less than "full enforcement". It is principally in this context that I too shall discuss it, despite the fact that, broadly stated, laws are not the overwhelming concern of front line uniformed police, whose duties are primarily of the non-law enforcement variety. To state that these duties also carry considerable elements of discretion is to state the obvious.

A policy of "full enforcement" implies that police are required to enforce all criminal statutes at all times against all offenders. It suggests that the police lack authority to ignore offences, to warn or counsel offenders when they have committed offences, to turn a "blind eye', or do anything short of either taking formal

[1] John R. Lambert, *Crime, Police and Race Relations* (London: Oxford University Press, 1970), p. 166.
[2] Banton, op. cit., p. 145.

notice of offences or arresting offenders. "It views the police
function to be that of relating the provisions of the law to a
fine measurement of the quantum of evidence. Out of this cold
and somewhat mechanical calculation evolves an answer which
provides the basis for police action."[3]

The exercise of discretion, on the other hand, suggests that
the police are required, because of several reasons, to decide:
how much of an effort is to be made to enforce specific laws
and what significance is to be attached to such laws; whether
the preservation of the public peace may be more effectively
served by ignoring minor breaches of the law; whether, in certain
cases, to counsel offenders in preference to invoking the criminal
process; what alternative police actions may achieve desired
goals; whether or not to prefer charges or make an arrest even
in those situations where both the offenders and the evidence
are at hand, and how and when a law should be enforced. It
tends to portray policemen as something more than automatons—
as reasonable men whose judgment is essential to determine the
issues with which they are confronted.

Some people cling to the view that the police should enforce
laws exactly and impartially, exercising no discretion whatever.
They deny the significance of discretion. Others grudgingly
concede that the exercise of sound and intelligent discretion for
effective police performance is necessary, but then somehow
stultify the concession by imagining all the abuses to which such
discretion could lead. Both groups somehow miscomprehend
both the nature of police work and police discretion in a
democracy. This is understandable, mainly because the reality of
the policeman's world is so often incomprehensible to the "out-
sider".

There are still others who accept that the police do and must
exercise discretion but lavishly expend their time criticising how
it is exercised. All views are valuable for one reason or another,
and police, who have a vital role in protecting freedom of speech,
must listen to other viewpoints and be prepared to adopt any they

[3] H. Goldstein, "Police Discretion: The Ideal versus the Real", *Public
Administrative Review* (September 1963), p. 140.

consider to be helpful. "However critics of the police are so very apt to assume that all police decisions are simple if only police would think as the critics do. Able-bodied critics are very welcome to put their theories to practical test."[4] "Insofar as academics cry out for a police who are everything to all men they are demanding the impossible."[5]

That police do exercise discretion is an inescapable fact. Police work in a democracy is largely an exercise in discretion. It is at the heart of the police role. Even though the criminal statutes vaguely imply that all laws, in all circumstances, and at all times are to be enforced, "what needs to be kept in mind is that police are not bound to prosecute all offenders of which they have knowledge".[6]

G. L. Williams quoting an English Attorney-General said: "It has never been the rule in this country that suspected criminals must automatically be the subject of prosecution. Public interest is the dominant consideration."[7] It is interesting to contrast this view with that of Christopher Williams[8] who pointed out that a constable's duty was to enforce the whole body of laws, breaches of which involve a penalty to be imposed in the criminal courts. He says that if police were entitled on their own initiative or someone else's to select which laws they are going to enforce and which to ignore, this would be unconstitutional. It would interpose between Parliament and the subject an agency over whose activities no control exists other than that provided by the courts.

For a number of reasons which will later emerge more fully, Christopher Williams' view is incompatible with the realities of police work in a democratic society. Yet one must try to understand, at least in part, why he, and perhaps others, take this view. By the time most criminal cases reach the calm

---

4 Frank Elmes, "Watch It", *Police Review* (6 August 1971), p. 1005.
5 Frank Elmes, "The Soul of Discretion", *Police Review* (30 April 1971), p. 550.
6 J. R. Lambert, op. cit., p. 164.
7 Quoted by J. R. Lambert, ibid., p. 164, from G. W. Williams, "Discretion in Prosecuting", *Criminal Law Review* (1956), p. 222.
8 *Criminal Law Review*, 1954, pp. 271-3.

atmosphere of a court, the facts in support of and surrounding the cases are, for the most part, neatly and unconfusingly arranged for ease of comprehension and to allow the truth to be recognised more clearly. Being divorced from the pre-trial police experience of trying to sort out what is often a mass of confused and distorted pieces of evidence in circumstances and under pressures which do not allow for analytical and dispassionate deliberation, it is so easy for courts and lawyers to take for granted that the orderly arrangement they see in front of them in court has always existed. This belief can cause them to see the exercise of police operational discretion as an uncomplicated task. "That a policeman's duties compel him to exercise personal discretion many times a day is evident. Crime does not look the same on the street as it does in a legislative chamber. How much noise or profanity makes conduct disorderly within the meaning of the law? When must a quarrel be treated as a criminal assault; at the first threat or at the first blow or after blood is drawn, or when a serious injury is inflicted?"[9]

The most notable occasion on which the exercise of discretion by police has been publicly aired was *R* v. *Metropolitan Police Commissioner ex parte Blackburn.* The applicant raised the question of the propriety of a policy decision in the London Metropolitan Police not to keep observation on gaming clubs for breach of the gaming laws unless there were complaints of cheating, or they had become the haunt of criminals. He also sought the remedy of mandamus against the Commissioner because the police failed to enforce the law in regard to gaming clubs.

Lord Denning[10] in the course of his judgment asserted: "Although the Chief Officers of the Police are answerable to the law, there are many fields in which they have a discretion with which the law will not interfere. For instance it is for the Chief Police Officer to decide in any particular case whether enquiries should be pursued or a prosecution brought." He goes on to say

---

[9] *The Challenge of Crime in a Free Society,* op. cit., p. 10.
[10] Quoted by A. F. C. Clissitt, "The Exercise of Discretion in the Enforcement of Law", *Police Review* (5 December 1969), p. 1082.

that the Chief Officer can make policy decisions and give effect to them, but there are some policy decisions which may amount to a neglect of duty with which the court can interfere. No member of the court denied that there was a discretion for the police to exercise, but at the same time they all affirmed that the result of such discretion could be challenged in the court in certain circumstances.

Why must discretion be exercised? We need to look first at the nature of the laws under which police operate and some of the social pressures which exist in our community.

The legislature has attempted to establish those forms of conduct which its members desire, on behalf of the community, to declare criminal. But many of these laws, either by intent to create greater flexibility in enforcement or as a result of limitations of language, are expressed in such broad terms as to render a clear intepretation of the legislation's intention most difficult. As Saunders correctly observed: "No code of conduct could possibly cover all circumstances in which policemen must make instantaneous and irrevocable decisions affecting human life and safety, property rights, and personal liberty. Such awesome responsibility for decision-making, indeed, sets the police apart from any other profession—after all, the physician may change his diagnosis, the lawyer his pleading. Decisions affecting human life cannot be made more wisely by reducing them to rote and removing police discretion entirely."[11] The policeman, unlike the judge, doctor, or the lawyer, often has to make up his mind on the spur of the moment with few reliable cues to help him. "Every legal rule, however clear and distinct its case may be, is vague at its periphery—a quality shared with all descriptive knowledge. Accordingly, in the determination of specific meanings, opinions differ."[12]

It is a fact that criminal laws are not always well suited to the human problems a policeman encounters. In part this explains why some laws are over-enforced while others are

---

[11] C. B. Saunders, *Upgrading the American Police* (Washington: The Brooking Institution, 1970), p. 25.

[12] Carl J. Friedrich, *Authority* (Nomas 1) (Harvard University Press, Cambridge, 1958), p. 63.

under-enforced. The law of assault, for example, is seldom invoked in the event of a family dispute. Policemen often prefer to exercise discretion for humanitarian reasons. Sometimes the public peace is best preserved by not enforcing the law. This is especially so at the scene of a demonstration where an attempt to enforce the law in certain circumstances, could lead to disorder. The policeman's oath requires him to prevent disorder but says nothing about "enforcing the law" as such.

"In order to determine the best course of action in any particular case, a policeman must be able to separate the sheep from the goats."[13] This may be easy for a country policeman. He usually knows the people. The city policeman, however, meets many people he has never seen before. This means that he can seldom predict how they will behave in the future. It is very important that he should have good judgment in handling them. He must remember too that he is dealing with human beings and not just laws. There is an obvious difference.

But even in the few cases where the law is quite clear in defining criminal conduct, there may be little expectation on the part of those who made the laws that they be enforced to the letter. The statute may be stating the ideals of the community at a particular time; that certain forms of illegal trading in liquor by sports clubs and certain forms of sexual activity, for example, will not be tolerated. Lawmakers and citizens alike may derive a certain degree of comfort from having legislated against such activity. Subsequently, should this false sense of comfort be a source of concern to the legislator, because of community opposition or changes in social values, he is faced with a dilemma. On the basis of political calculation he is more inclined to take a passive, non-committal stance than to be caught supporting the repeal of such a prohibition. Police then have to live with the law, even though the grounds upon which it was made in the first place have long disappeared. Many of the provisions of the Police Offences Act are a good example of this obsolescence.

There is a view which suggests that where the law is confused or outmoded or even stupid, its very enforcement by the police

---

[13] Banton, op. cit., p. 139.

with the attendant publicity, is more likely to ensure its revision or repeal. This view ignores the fact that police, because of the very nature of their duties, are totally dependent on public co-operation and support. Enforcing, or being publicly identified (as police inescapably are) with, laws which the public regard as harmless, outmoded, or of no great consequence in physically protecting people or their property or which were created to support values that have since ceased to be important, is a rapid means of bringing about alienation of the public and thus impedes police efforts to protect the public against the more hurtful and menacing forms of crime. So often, the difficulties between police and citizens arise from a clash in perception of what is valued, i.e. what is right or wrong. If a segment of the public feels highly aggrieved today because of police enforcement of trifling or outmoded laws, it is likely to withdraw its support tomorrow—perhaps at a time when that support is required by police to prevent or detect crime. No other agency within the system of administration of justice faces this dilemma to the same extent as the police. A judge or magistrate can inflict what-ever penalty is allowed by law but after doing so he does not have to go out and face the community at an operational and personal level and seek its active support.

It is therefore very important that politicians are mindful of the implications which disliked legislation can have in terms of police-community relations. They should take care not to place, or allow to remain in the law, powers and duties which can lead to greater difficulties for the police in maintaining good public relations. But they must be convinced that that is the situation. Even then a powerful minority may still wish to retain a generally unpopular law. Legislators, too, should choose the enforcement agency with care. It may be that a certain category of generally unpopular but essential laws should be enforced by an enforce-ment agency which is less reliant on good public relations than the police.

The extent to which the legislative requirement for police to enforce certain and largely unpopular "private morality" and "pornographic" laws—often at the cost of reducing manpower resources needed in other and perhaps more important tasks—

alienates public support for police, could be a useful subject for future research. On this score Morris and Hawkins castigated the American police: "Why are there no strong police voices for a retrenchment of our moralistic criminal law? Why do the police not argue: let us protect you, not coddle your spurious virtue. Why are they not dedicated to achieving a more modestly phrased but socially effective criminal law, aiming to protect us as far as it can from physical violence and certain serious property degradations—and little else? In the morals area they so readily put on the priestly garb. . . . We overload them with morally pretentious law, and require them to demonstrate wisdom and skill higher than expected of any of the established professions."[14]

Similarly a *Dominion* editorial of 24 March 1972 rebuked the New Zealand police: "Ten good men and two good women have struck a blow for permissiveness in the theatre that should keep Mother Grundy quiet for a long time to come. . . . Indeed it seems incredible to liberal New Zealanders that a prosecution should ever be launched. But it was. The police, showing the traditional concern for Mother Grundy's state of mind that led them into the Dr. Greer prosecution decided they had a case. The Attorney-General, Sir Roy Jack, concurred. . . The police should now feel free to stop acting like puppets on strings held by self appointed guardians of outmoded moral standards. They should be glad to be able to devote more of their time and energy to more important duties. People concerned about the change in moral standards would not be deprived of the opportunity to test public opinion. They can always conduct private prosecution."

There is no doubt that the volume of public thinking on the question of how much discretion police should use in enforcing "moral" laws, whether they should be enforcing these laws at all, or even whether some of them should exist, is increasing. This controversy shows the complexity of the police role in today's questioning society.

---

[14] N. Morris and G. Hawkins, *The Honest Politician's Guide to Crime Control* (University of Chicago Press, 1970), pp. 88-89.

Laws which do not meet with wide community supports are very difficult to enforce—at least in a practical sense. Witnesses are reluctant to come forward and when they do, they run the risk of being socially ostracised. Clearly, if police do not present their views in respect of "unenforceable" laws no one will do it for them. Only the police fully appreciate the day-to-day problems of being "on the street" and the intricacies of their daily relations with the public. It could be argued that this expertise should not be ignored and its benefit lost to the public.

New Zealand police periodically suggest changes in the law. Whether this should be done more often is difficult to decide. Police face this dilemma: on the one hand, they do not want to appear dabblers in politics or underminers of the formal concept of ministerial responsibility; on the other hand, they realise that silence is not always a virtue. "Nowadays there is no such thing as dignified silence. The assumption of the public is that there is no case to answer."[15] That a particular law is unpopular with a section or certain segments of the community is not, by itself, a sufficient reason to justify change. Nor should police act as the spearhead in effecting changes in the criminal law, unless such a law manifestly hampers the ability of police to effectively carry out their work. Where there is a police need to complain about bad laws, it is important that proper procedures and channels are followed in doing so.

So far I have examined police discretion mainly within the context of the law and some of the implications which certain types of laws can have for police community relations. Police discretion, however, cannot be properly evaluated without considering other sources from which policemen draw their ideas about how and when to exercise discretion. Apart from their training, the example of their colleagues, the tradition of the service, the department's policies, the constraints on scarce manpower resources, and the expressions of opinion heard in courts, other sources are especially influential.

Policemen derive much of their sense of judgment from experi-

[15] *Dominion* editorial, 3 March 1972.

ences of their private lives. Kaufman[16] noted that men do not enter organisations devoid of opinions, values, preferences, and their own interpretations of the world; nor do they shed all of these once they become members. True, these things may be modified by organisational experience. Job experience however is only part of a person's total experience. Many of the pre-dilections or prejudices each policeman brings with him to his work persist in some degree even when they are not in harmony with the desires and objectives of his organisational leaders. Still, overseas studies and my own police experience tend to show that different problems in the actual police work situation are probably more decisive in shaping police behaviour and ideology than pre-service or private experiences.

Out of uniform, the New Zealand policeman is subject to much the same influences as any other citizen. In mixing with other citizens he soon hears what they think of the police and this influences many of his decisions. If he loses touch with public sentiment he cannot use his discretion wisely. This is one of the strongest reasons why there should always be close and friendly relations between police and all sections of the community, the law-abiding as well as those labelled the opposite. Society itself is inclined to set the so-called criminal class apart as being some-thing different and less deserving of social and humane recogni-tion. Policemen must avoid falling into this trap. People labelled "criminal" make up a proportion of the policeman's clientele but their main distinguishing mark is that they have been identified as breachers of the law. What of those who have not been so identified—what is known as the "dark figure"? Overseas studies would suggest that the latter group exceeds the former.

To a large extent police discretion is governed more by popular morality than the letter of the law. Popular morality as it affects the police can be recognised in Rice's argument "that any given organisation 'imports' various things from its environment, utilises these imports in some kind of 'conversion' process, and then 'exports' . . . services . . . which result from the conversion

---

[16] H. Kaufman, *The Forest Ranger: A Study in Administrative Behaviour* (Maryland: John Hopkins Press, 1960), p. 80.

process. One key import is the information obtained from the environment pertaining to the primary task—that is, what the organisation must do in order to survive."[17] Popular morality, too, is reflected in the quality of service which police provide. As Elmes noted: ". . . a brash, brutal society as in Nazi Germany will produce a brash brutal police; a strong authoritarian society, as in Stalin's Russia, will produce a strong authoritarian police; a radically divided society will produce a police showing exactly those prejudices; a permissive society will produce a police even more unsure of its role; so the variables go on."[18]

Finally, there is the pragmatic element which influences police discretion. Being a microcosm of the society they serve, policemen in New Zealand come from and are part of a society which practices and believes in the pragmatic approach. The strict interpreter is not appreciated. While society may accept the need for the enforcement of a particular law at the same time it usually expects humane police action. One suspects that the use of discretion in making public decisions is at the very heart of the national temperament. How then could the police function without using discretion and yet retain public support?

It must not be inferred from what has been said that the New Zealand police have unlimited discretion or even that they apply their discretionary freedom to the extent that perhaps they should do. Obviously what the community regards as serious or violent crime will invite firm police action but the police must still act within the rule of law and in accordance with humane principles, despite any public emotionalism and utterances that might insist otherwise.

Police are generally permitted to exercise more discretion in self-initiated activity than in events initiated by citizens' complaints. It is easy, however, to use public complaints as a justification for strict enforcement of the law. Complaints from a member or members of the public may, in some circumstances, be no justification. The public seldom sees the wider social and

[17] E. H. Schein, *Organisational Psychology* (2nd ed.) (Prentice-Hall Inc., Englewood Cliffs, N.J., 1965), p. 107.
[18] F. Elmes, "Where the Fault Lies", *Police Review,* 26 June 1970, p. 671.

human considerations and implications of taking or not taking a person to court. Nor do they always report matters to the police from motives of civic mindedness; public vindictiveness and unreasonable conservativeness are not unknown. In any case, merely because a member of the public complains of an offence, there is no legal or moral obligation on the police to take the offender to court. This is as it should be. Each case must be judged on its merits. Making this judgment carries with it a grave responsibility as well as an obligation of service to the public. As Disraeli observed: "All power is a trust, we are accountable for its exercise—that, from the people and for the people, all springs, and all must exist."[19]

The police dilemma is to try to balance efficiency with apparent impartiality. But if "impartiality" is given its popular meaning of "acting in the same way to everyone and treating all alike" then, in the context of police work or of any other work, impartiality is merely an ideal, rather than a realistic expectation. The circumstances of each incident handled by the police are unique. So too are the circumstances of each offender. The police oath requires policemen to "try to the best of their ability" to be impartial. "The impartial conduct which officers are officially expected to display often seems unsuited to the realities of human interaction under stressful street conditions, a sympathetic observer can easily understand the frustrations felt by officers under these trying conditions. Perhaps we are asking police officers to do something that is beyond the capacity of ordinary mortals."[20]

The fear of being seen as not impartial has acted as a powerful motivator behind the traditional refusal of policemen to openly acknowledge that police discretion is, and has always been, used, or to extend the use of discretion. Happily, this tradition was recently broken by the New Zealand Commissioner of Police. He issued for the guidance of all policemen written criteria for

[19] *Oxford Dictionary of Quotations* (Oxford University Press, London, 1956), p. 1.
[20] N. A. Watson and J. W. Sterling, *Police and Their Opinions* (Washington: International Association of Chiefs of Police, 1969), p. 3.

discretionary judgment in police handling of a wide variety of offences. These criteria gained considerable favourable public response through the mass media. One could conclude from the favourable public response that policemen have in the past underestimated the ability of the community to appreciate the need for wide police discretion.

Goldstein, a policeman himself, in explaining the reluctance of police administrators to publicly acknowledge that discretion is used, said: "He (the police administrator) is most likely to suport the view—somewhat hesitatingly—that he is committed to a policy of full enforcement. It is, after all, the policy most enunciated by police agencies. In contrast, the mere suggestion that a police administrator exercises discretion in fulfilling his job may be taken as an affront—an attack upon the objective and sacrosanct nature of his job—that of enforcing the law without favour. . . Like planned parenthood, it may be something you practice; it is not something you admit or even discuss. . . . And yet in acknowledging that some or all of these practices exist, police officials feel a sense of guilt; that these actions are not quite proper; and that they had no basis in law. . . . Another contention is that discretion breeds corruption and for this reason should be denied. . . . The average police administrator spends a considerable portion of his time worrying about the integrity of his force. . . . The whole thought of trying to defend a policy of selective enforcement is a bit frightening. . . . So he often concludes that it is, in his opinion, much safer to maintain he has no discretion in these matters."[21]

The uneasiness described by Goldstein and which has pervaded the thoughts of New Zealand police administrators has not been helped by the now largely obsolete, but still extant, piece of legal philosophy stated by Luxford S.M.: "One person may only suffer directly from a breach of the criminal law; but the law moves independently of that person's wishes, once it is set in motion. A person who has reported an offence to the police may regret his action, but on trying to stop further proceedings learns that it is

[21] H. Goldstein, "Police Discretion: The Ideal Versus the Real". *Public Administration Review* (September 1963), p. 140.

too late. Indeed, the expression 'it is in the hands of the police', and its well-known effect, has given rise to the suggestion that the force is a soul-less, relentless body that never lets up until the law has been vindicated. . . . A breach of the criminal law affects the whole community, and, upon proof in due form, the offender MUST [my emphasis] be punished as a warning to persons in general that the law must be obeyed."[22]

We come now to the question of control over police discretion. American legal writers pursue this aspect with inordinate vigour, especially in regard to checks against its abuse. The social forces giving rise to such abuse receive less attention. The few excursions which New Zealand law students have made into this field have invariably followed the American trail, both in content and style.

That there is a need for constant alertness to ensure that there is no unfairness in the use of police discretion cannot be denied. This is the mark of a democratic society. But despite the apprehension usually exhibited by the judiciary and legal profession against possible abuses of police discretion, it is fair comment to say that no state servants are publicly scrutinised to the same extent as that which is endured and accepted by the New Zealand police. Police activities in relation to crime detection receive more publicity from the "hungry" mass media and a vitally interested public than those in any other state department or commercial venture. The effectiveness of this type of control over the use of police discretion needs no elucidation.

Let us for a moment reflect on the courts as a means of control. Apart from policemen, what other state servants have their decisions, at least a good many of them, subjected to judicial enquiry and by a process of cross-examination in courts under the watchful eyes of the bench, press, lawyers, social welfare workers, court officials, and the general public? One could ask: if members of the judiciary and the legal profession—incidentally, both groups are outside the Ombudsman's jurisdiction—were to have the elements of their decision-making exercises subjected

---

[22] J. H. Luxford, *Police Law in New Zealand* (2nd ed.) (Wellington: Butterworth & Co. Ltd., 1950), pp. 2-3.

to the type of scrutiny earlier described, what would be the result? Prudence would dictate that this question is best left unanswered.

It can be argued that many police discretionary judgments are beyond the reach of the courts and mass media, especially where they are not determined by specific legislative mandates. What controls then exist? Perhaps one of the most potent controlling devices of all is that front-line police work, unlike the work of many state servants, is conducted in situations where there is an immediate and personal interaction with members of a sensitive and well enlightened public, who are increasingly conscious of their civil and human rights and who have easy access to the news media. "The power of the public is effective power. It is effective power because the role performance of policemen is both highly observable and easily confronted by public sanction. The observability of their role activities stems directly from their conspicuous occupational front—the uniform, the badge, and the marked car—and indirectly through public reports, courts of law, and legislative bodies."[23]

The controlling devices already mentioned do not include: the legal remedies that exist in law to challenge the use of police discretion; the powers of the Ombudsman to investigate police administrative decisions, the prerogative of any M.P. to question police actions during parliamentary "question time"; or what Sir Thaddeus McCarthy[24] described as the "finely constructed disciplinary system designed to encourage a high standard and to punish breaches". All of these aside, top police administrators realise that well selected, well trained and supervised policemen, who have a strong moral and social consciousness, are the best public assurance against abuse of police discretion.

Controls can be taken too far. They are subject to the law of diminishing returns. Workers who are supervised too closely tend to concentrate on satisfying the supervisor instead of getting on with the job. There is no reason why policemen should be any

[23] J. J. Preiss, H. J. Ehrlich, *An Examination of Role Theory* (*The Case of the State Police*) (University of Nebraska Press, 1966), p. 124.
[24] The Rt. Hon. Sir Thaddeus McCarthy, op. cit., p. 176.

different. "No matter how well trained he is, no matter what guidelines he works under, no matter how close his supervision is, the majority of the police officer's decisions will be characterised by a measure of subjectivity, idiosyncratic selection and ideological interpretation in defining a given situation."[25]

In the exercise of discretion, policemen have made, do make, and will continue to make mistakes. Mistakes are inevitable in a field concerned with the vagaries of human conduct. This is obvious. What may not be so obvious is that mistakes, once they are identified as such, should be frankly admitted. To do so not only shows moral integrity and honesty but, in general, it also brings a sympathetic public response—probably because the community has been conditioned not to expect state servants to openly admit their misjudgments. Once they discover exceptions, they are both agreeably surprised and tend to see their own human weaknesses reflected in the bureaucracy.

All the signs suggest that in coming years the decisions of the front-line policemen will be increasingly subject to scrutiny. The public demands upon their sense of judgment will mount. They will need to be seen more as persuaders or motivators than coercers. In this way, their basic discretion is more important than that used by high ranking officers considering cases submitted to them in writing. "The police department has a special property (shared with few other organisations) that within it, discretion increases as one moves down the hierarchy."[26] ". . . The beat patrolman in a congested high crime rate area is called upon to make highly sophisticated judgments having a major impact on the lives of the individuals involved. Such judgments are not mechanical in nature, they are every bit as complicated as the decisions made by any of the behavioural scientists and in many cases are more difficult because they must be made under the pressure of immediate circumstances."[27]

[25] Neiderhoffer, op. cit., p. 5.
[26] G. E. Berkley, *The Democratic Policeman* (Boston: Beacon Press, 1969), p. 182.
[27] *Task Force Report: The Police, the President's Commission on Law Enforcement and Administration of Justice* (U.S. Government Printer, 1967), p. 26.

Emerging from these considerations is the conclusion that the operational and social setting, including the nature of the laws[28] and community characteristics and pressures exert considerable influence on how and why New Zealand policemen exercise discretion. In each situation the policeman's judgment is largely contingent upon a complex set of factors other than simply behaviour against the law. How each situation is handled is also dictated by humane considerations rather than inflexible adherence to abstract principles of the law which often bear little relationship to reality. Every intelligent policeman becomes aware of the distinction between what is expected by the book and what will be expected and tolerated by his community, superiors, and peers. Inevitably he exercises his discretion not in a vacuum but in an environment which is surrounded by a web of interests, a web sometimes dominated by the unpredictable spider. Still, it is this environment which makes his tasks not only demanding, but also challenging and rewarding.

[28] For an excellent analysis of the harmful effects which certain criminal laws may have on police-community relations see Cameron, "Some Consequences of an Overextended Criminal Law" in Clark, ed., *Essays on Criminal Law in New Zealand* (1971), pp. 158-162.

5

Concept of Police Efficiency and Effectiveness

Within the police "efficiency" is an oft-used word. As we will see it is too diffuse a concept to be susceptible to any cut-and-dried definition. In business, efficiency is normally measured by the relationship between value of output and the costs of production. An efficient firm is usually believed to be one where there is a favourable relationship between the two.

What does efficiency mean in the context of police work? In 1829, Richard Mayne and Charles Rowan, who were the first commissioners of the London Metropolitan police, expounded the since-famous test of police efficiency: "To recognise always that the test of police efficiency is the absence of crime and disorder, and not the visible evidence of police action in dealing with them."[1] To my knowledge this mythical test of police efficiency has gone unchallenged. Yet one has only to reflect on the crime rate in, say, a "mature" middle-class suburban area such as Khandallah, with that of a similar sized and populated new urban area such as Porirua, to appreciate that the absence or presence of crime is a misleading guide to police efficiency. Burns had a point when he said: "Myths change more slowly than reality. In a sense a myth is a contradiction—and when un-related to changing reality—helps to build up a completely false

---

[1] Charles Reith, *A New Study of Police History* (London: Oliver and Boyde, 1956), p. 288.

73

concept that is almost invulnerable to rational argument. As a result, actions based on changing reality seem immoral . . . to those whose perceptions are still dominated by outdated myths. . . ."[2]

It is instructive to study Saunders'[3] view which not only demolishes the efficiency test advocated by Rowan and Mayne, but also provides further insights into the concept of police effectiveness. He says: "Any discussions of problems of police quality and quantity is made more difficult by the inadequacies of existing criteria for evaluating police effectiveness. The usual measures—authorised strength, equipment, and trends in crime statistics—do not take full account of the realities of the police task and fail to measure the quality and competence of personnel. . . . The question is not how many bodies, but how many trained men are available. . . . The effectivness of manpower will always depend on the quality of the personnel. . . . The relationship between the quality and amount of police activity and the rate of crime or the conviction of offenders is not predictable. The size and quality of a police force may have comparatively little effect on the prevalence of crime compared with other factors such as size, make up, and density of population, geography, climate and economic and social characteristics of the region. Probably the chief factor is population—its age, sex, race, and particularly its economic status."

Banton[4] says that "in the case of certain occupations it is fairly easy to agree on criteria of organisational efficiency. . . ." He explains that the police have to meet "many criteria and it is difficult to compare the value of success in one direction at the expense of shortcomings in another. For example, a police force which solved more crimes but which treated suspects with undue severity would be in one sense more efficient, but its practices would incite public protest. The police are given a variety of objectives but they are simultaneously subjected to a host of

[2] H. Burns (Jr.), "Tampering with Myths", *Canadian Journal of Criminology and Corrections* (Vol. 13, No. 2), April 1971, p. 129.

[3] C. B. Saunders, *Upgrading the American Police* (Washington: The Brooking Institution, 1970), pp. 61-65.

[4] Banton, op. cit., pp. 105-106.

restrictions concerning the ways in which they may attain them, and the interplay between ends and means is much more complex than in most organisations."

In an organisation like the police whose output is not material, statements about effectiveness and efficiency are extremely difficult. If the community were to put pressure on the police to increase their efficiency by prosecuting more burglars, this could be done by using inhumane methods. Could the police then be regarded as effective or efficient? Likewise if policeman "A" handles a sudden death or family dispute in a sympathetic, consolatory and humane manner and policeman "B" detects a burglar through careful inquiries—then, which policeman is more effective or efficient? The latter's effort only will be reflected in the police annual report to Parliament. How can the intelligent and responsible exercise of police discretion, the fairness with which laws are enforced or the policeman's qualities of mind and character and the adequacy of his training be measured? How can that feeling of social well-being, enjoyed by citizens when they see a nearby constable patrolling the area in which they live, be measured? Obviously, these are aspects which cannot be measured. Yet they are no less important than the crime clearance rate.

Currently, we see that cost-benefit analysis, operations research, and programme budgeting are fashionable tools for effective organisational decision-making. Useful though these tools may be, they have been developed without explicit consideration to what Professor Wildavsky calls "exchange costs and hostility costs", or what Nuestadt refers to as "reputation costs".[5] These costs are of vital importance to the police department.

It may be that the efficiency of the police may "be less important than their responsiveness to the community that they are required to serve".[6] "Men who think first and foremost of efficiency and conceive of it in narrow terms are seldom demo-

[5] A. Wildovsky, "The Political Economy of Efficiency: Cost-Benefit Analysis, System Analysis, and Programme Budgeting", *Public Administration Review,* 1966 (26: 292-310), p. 309.
[6] Banton, op. cit., p. 106.

crats."[7] "Efficiency, it is true, is a major objective of public administration, but it must be socially and humanely interpreted. Efficiency is a matter of quality, and hence quantitative and mechanical methods of measurements must perforce be far from complete."[8]

There is widespread agreement that the success of the police in carrying out their preventive and protective functions in a democratic state are dependent on their ability to gain and maintain community support and respect. If this statement is accepted, as indeed it must, then there is a strong argument for suggesting that police effectiveness or efficiency should, for the most part, be judged on the basis of the amount of community support and respect which exist for the police. Police efficiency and effectiveness in this sense must involve multiple criteria, including the quality of police candidates, police education and training; ability of police to react with flexibility to changing environmental demands; police ability to mobilise community action in eliminating the causes of crime; communication and leadership within the police; police commitment to the rule of law in carrying out in a humane manner a diverse range of activities; police ability to help in keeping crime at a tolerable level without unduly infringing upon individual freedom; and the degree of public acceptability for laws which are enforced by police. It is true also that community support is intangible, and thus devoid of precise measurement. It can, however, be assessed on a day-to-day basis by the amount of police-citizen tension, conflict, harmony, or co-operation which exists, together with the public attitudes shown towards police and which are reflected in the mass media, courts, and in other diverse ways. Using the degree of community support and respect as a key element in evaluating police efficiency and effectiveness, has obvious advantages for both police and public.

It creates a desirable degree of police sensitivity towards its various publics and in effect forces the police to attempt to

---

[7] A. D. Lindsay, *The Modern Democratic State* (London: Oxford University Press, 1943), p. 140.
[8] Dwight Waldo, *The Administrative State* (New York, The Ronald Press Co., 1948), p. 197.

identify and alleviate those obstacles, internal or external, which militate against maintaining community support and respect. The external aspects for example may include, among other things, laws which have lost their consonance with every-day moral assumptions or which have been outpaced by public morality. The internal aspects would include defective attitudes of members of the police in their relations with members of the public. When the public have genuine complaints against the police, seldom are they concerned about the police action taken; rather they complain about the attitude of policemen. "The term 'attitude' itself is vague, yet it seems the best way to express a very simple thing—the state of mind which lies behind everything we do. It is theoretically possible for an individual to operate efficiently with a bad attitude, but in the long run he will be hurting himself and his associates—and ultimately he will wreck the mission of the organisation. If proper attitude is essential for the ordinary individual in everyday life, it is more than ever important for the individual policeman."[9] The question of attitudes needs to be taken a little further.

The late L. J. Rathgen, when Commissioner of the Inland Revenue Department, is credited with having been largely responsible for the development within and outside his department of a new and healthier attitude towards taxation. McAllister says:[10] "In Rathgen's words: '. . . The old idea was to be efficient in the narrowest sense and indeed without any particular consideration for the social . . . need of the democratic community. . . . Effectiveness in the broad sense in all public administration is more calculated to preserve our democratic way of life. Efficiency in the cold, hard attitudeless sense could involve hardship, inhumane decisions and injustices. . . . The public official should constantly seek to put himself in the position of the citizen with whom he is dealing. He should remember that the citizen cannot fail to be sensitive to the manner in which the public official treats him. . . . The citizen has a right to expect,

---

[9] R. La Couture, "The Police, The Press, and Public Relations", *Police* (September-October, 1961), p. 44.
[10] D. McAllister, "The Philosophy of Administrator L. J. Rathgen", *N.Z.J.P.A.* (September 1966), pp. 37-62.

not only that his affairs will be dealt with effectively and expeditiously, but also that his personal feelings, no less than his rights as an individual, will be sympathetically and fairly considered. . . . If one has attitudes which are not based on a reverence of the needs of humanity, or for principles of good-will and understanding, these too, are a bar to good public service'."

Rathgen's underlying philosophy of *Service and Understanding* and his strong conviction for the fundamental worth of the individual is surely based on what Barclay[11] described as "the topmost peak of social ethics and the Everest of all ethical teaching", namely: "Do to others what you would have them do to you." If this formula is applied and the public responses are then assessed in terms of community co-operation and respect, we finish up with two elements—each being dependent on the other. First, an operating philosophy and secondly, a way of judging the results of that philosophy. There seems undoubted merit in using both as the main criteria for evaluating police effectiveness or efficiency.

[11] Rev. W. Barclay, *The Gospel of Matthew,* p. 280.

6

The Police Role Re-defined:
Some Considerations for the Future

This final chapter will recapitulate briefly the thrust and implications of the arguments developed so far and re-define the broad
functional role of the New Zealand police.

Basic to any meaningful police-community partnership in the
task of maintaining a civilised society in a democracy is the need
to delineate the police role so that there are reasonable expectations and understandings about what the police can do, should
do, and are allowed to do.

Historically, even though the police role was not accurately
articulated, no one seemed unduly concerned. This is not now the
case. Today's mobile and urban-centred society, with its greater
diversity and volume of political and social opinion; with its
reluctance to accept governmental or police determination of
what is right and wrong in relation to moral conduct; with its
declining reliance on the traditional and religious forms of social
control; with its tendency to believe that police should have the
cure for crime; with its increasing eagerness to scrutinise and
humanise decisions made by state servants; creates an atmosphere in which public conflict and interest over the rationale
for, and effectiveness of, police action becomes a matter of major
importance.

For police in these circumstances to leave the old definition of
the police role unclarified is to ignore their social responsibility.
Their antennae must be intelligently sensitive so that they can

respond to public signals, otherwise they cannot hope to secure and maintain co-operation. This does not mean that they should try to bend to every whim of a modern, and so-called "permissive society". The public is seldom fully informed and is often divided in its opinions.

I see the need for, and the development of, a growing community and political awareness that the maintenance of law and order is not simply a matter of enough police backed by punitively-minded courts. There is no intent here to deprecate the importance of having sufficient policemen to help in protecting the community. But for too long, the community, the Government and the police themselves have tended increasingly to view crime prevention, detection, and control as a sole police responsibility. This is an "impossible" mandate for any one agency in a democracy. Not only does it cause police to be judged by a standard they cannot meet, but when citizens experience increased crime and disorder, significant numbers of them come to feel a loss of trust and confidence in the police. Police ability to protect people diminishes as the gulf between the police and community widens. "When one is responsible for 'everything', one is also vulnerable for the inevitable mistakes in carrying out the impossible. That is the heart of the policeman's lot."[1]

So often the public fail to realise that crime is a social phenomenon, a symptom of ills within society which cannot be cured by the police. Society itself is creating an environment which breeds crime and disorder. It then asks policemen to efficiently control its effects and while doing so to pay scrupulous attention to the rights of suspects and offenders. These are conflicting demands—a fact about which criminologists appear to be silent. A consequence of this is that when militant proponents of civil rights gain a voice powerful enough to over-influence society, a great many criminals who might justly be subject to the judicial process, are exempt from it. When this happens the individual rights of victims of crime, and the necessity for order within society, are neglected. As far as I can ascertain, such

---

[1] Arthur Niederhoffer and Abraham S. Blumberg, *The Police in Social and Historical Perspective* (New York: Ginn & Company, 1970), p. 15.

proponents have not put forward any practical remedies which would help the community to prevent and detect crime. If they were to do so, they would command the respect of policemen.

Maintaining law and order in a democracy is a shared responsibility. "This idea of collective responsibility of the community for the maintenance of law and order and the responsibility of the individual not only to keep the law but also to see that it is kept by others, is one of the cardinal constitutional principles that has come down unbroken from Anglo-Saxon times to the present day."[2] This principle is still valid and is one of the main keys in keeping a democracy governable by democratic means. It is a principle which should never be neglected, as it has been, in the curricula of our schools, colleges, and universities, and in the homes, churches, and workplaces. It makes sound sense in a society which values freedom from crime, disorder and enforced conformity. Unfortunately, the principle does not seem to be fully appreciated by the larger community.

Despite the increasing trend for the development of specialised divisions of labour in society, no one agency can have, or assume to have, a monopoly on crime prevention and control. This is especially so in an urban, mobile, and democratic society.

More and more people must come to realise that the police are but one segment in our social structure and in their traditional role, can do little more than attempt to cope with the results of crime. Many of their gains and setbacks are closely tied up with the complex cross-currents in the larger society. Indeed many factors are believed to be more important than the presence of the police in influencing the absence or growth of crime and disorder. They include: the strength of the social control systems in the home, school, church, and workplace; the way cities are planned; the quality of laws and the influence of the news media; population stratification and density; and the socio-economic status of groups in society. No doubt, there are many other unidentified factors.

Peace in a free society must depend on voluntary compliance

[2] Colonel Sir Eric St. Johnston, "The British Police Experience", *The Police Journal,* November 1969, p. 490.

with the law. Indeed, the whole concept of keeping the peace in a democratic society rests on the assumption that a co-operative public acts as a substitute for the omnipresent policeman. The primary responsibility for upholding the law therefore lies not with the police, but with the people. This is evinced by the fact that in our society the great majority of crimes investigated by the police are reported initially by members of the public. In a democratic society, there is scarcely any other way in which to discover the commission of crimes. In the same way, very few crimes can be prevented, detected, or proven in court, without the immediate involvement of members of the public. The position would be different in a totalitarian state where police, supposedly, have such unlimited powers that technical limitations are the only restraints upon the tactics which they can employ to maintain law and order. For police to be effective crime controllers in such a state, there is no need for them to depend on the public for support and good-will.

I see the development of a new image for the front-line policeman as the public conception of his role is changed from a "catch-you" orientation, to a "people and service" orientation with policemen using their discretion wisely in resolving conflict and in meeting human service responsibilities. In fact I see all frontline police duties being recognised as a wide and diverse variety of welfare service, to both the individual and to society itself.

The service posture will break with the traditional and erroneous public conception that equates police action with "arrest" and "crime fighting". Such a concept concentrates on a small but very necessary portion of normal police duties. What seems a false dichotomy between "social work" and "police work" will be resolved in the minds of policemen. The total volume of duties carried out by the police adds up to a vast and almost unmanageable social domain. It can be argued that the historical definition of the police role was so broad and vague that it achieved this regrettable result by creating the belief that police could function as a surrugate service agency handling the multi-needs of the community anytime and anywhere, and with each policeman being all things to all people.

To claim that policemen should be concerned only with crime and enforcing the law is unrealistic. The human emergencies which police are asked to deal with, do not divide themselves neatly into categories that are crime-related or not crime-related. What is not generally realised is that all Government departments necessarily enforce laws within their areas of speciality. With the prolification and growing complexity of laws, it would be impossible for today's policeman to act as society's sole or main law enforcer.

In practice, society largely determines what the policeman does on a day-to-day basis. Very little front-line police action is initiated by policemen themselves; rather it is initiated by members of the public asking the police to "do something". If, for argument's sake, policemen were allowed to restrict themselves to enforcing laws only, their image would undoubtedly suffer. If policemen are over-identified with criminal proceedings, their relations with the public suffer. Public co-operation is enhanced and the quality of life improved when the police and the public are able to enjoy as many positive contacts with each other as circumstances permit. Such contacts help policemen to secure community co-operation in solving serious crime. (They also have the effect of encouraging policemen to exercise discretion in the performance of their duties.)

It can be argued then, that duties which militate against the police image—e.g. collecting money (fines) owing to the Courts, and civil debt money on behalf of solicitors—and which are unrelated to the peace-keeping, crime prevention/detection, and the protective role of policemen, should be performed by an agency less dependent than the police on public co-operation.

If we accept, as indeed we must, that the effectiveness of police in helping to preserve a peaceful democratic society, is largely dependent on their ability to create a public opinion in favour of co-operating with the police, then any strategy which has the effect of bringing police and other agencies together to pursue crime prevention goals is extremely worthwhile. Indeed this concept could well be practised by periodically training social workers and policemen together, in one institution. This would have the effect of: reducing conflicting operating ideologies and ignorance of the others' operations; helping policemen to learn from social workers some of the concepts which would assist in their understanding of different social problems and the people affected by them; help social workers to absorb the policeman's "reality therapy" and appreciate some of the problems he is asked to deal with—often in inflammable situations which are far removed from the comparatively unhurried, calm, and safe environment experienced by social workers. In short, joint training efforts could not only give police and social workers insight and sensitivity into the other's work but could also produce a more co-ordinated and co-operative problem-solving system.

I see the development of inter-agency team work in which policemen, probation officers, social workers, clergymen, community welfare officers of the Internal Affairs department, local authority welfare officers, community volunteers, members of the legal profession operating in the welfare field, and other social welfare agencies—whether governmental or otherwise—will periodically come together at a district level, share their problems, watch the built-in social mechanisms for maintaining order to see that they work as well as possible, plan joint social welfare programmes, and operate by way of a united front in dealing with social ills likely to breed crime and disorder. Because police are often the first of the social services to have anti-social behaviour drawn to their attention, they are in a good position to initiate police-citizen team efforts.

Through this concerted and unified approach, more effective solutions may be found. But implicit in this approach is the development of a model of the social environment in which we live. Police can contribute substantially to this model. Because of their position in society, they have access to data which reflect on many aspects of urban life. For example, an analysis of calls for police assistance could be used to:

   (i) identify conditions which may be contributing to crime and delinquency, and

  (ii) identify the range and type of essential social services which are not available after 5 p.m.

(iii) initiate, stimulate, and assist the development of programmes aimed at alleviating such conditions.

(iv) assist in providing a more effective performance by other agencies, both voluntary and governmental.

Most importantly, such analysis could lead to a more rational allotment of community responsibilities for what are now commonly thought of as police problems only.

The development of inter-agency team work has many other advantages. "By increasing the number of constructive interactions between policemen and citizens, their knowledge and trust of one another increases. The productive relationship is not confined to the supply of information alone. It makes the citizen more responsive to what the policeman has to tell him as well. Thus, a welcome cycle of beneficial interaction can be established."[3]

Improving police-public relations involves a constant re-examination of fundamental attitudes. Police must listen patiently and understandingly to people who are openly critical of them, since those people are precisely the ones with whom relations need to be improved. The time has arrived when those interest groups, who tend to criticise police actions, must be fully acquainted with the practical realities of police work, even taken in to police confidence, and asked to contribute their ideas on how police can more effectively deal with community problems. Although such groups cannot be expected to present cure-all ideas, less uninformed criticism and a substantial flow of good-will is the likely result.

I see the police striving to achieve professional recognition but at the same time avoiding estrangement from the community. Professional recognition must have as its essential base, not only an emphasis on organisational and technical efficiency, but more importantly, on a firm commitment to providing a humane, people-orientated, legal and protective service for all citizens irrespective of who or where they are and with an unwavering preoccupation with, and regard for, personal rights and liberties.

[3] Berkley, op. cit., p. 183.

The extent to which police achieve professional recognition will also depend on the quality of their recruits, their training, their brand of internal leadership, their effectiveness as communicators, how they use their discretion, their ability to understand and respond humanely to the needs of society and the often confusing and multi-level messages it despatches.

As an outcome of what I have said so far, I see a need for the broad functional role of the police to be recognised and defined more in these terms:

(a) To provide services within the legal framework and in consideration for the social values and aspirations of a democratic society in order to *help the community:*

    (i) To prevent crime and protect life and property, by guarding, patrolling and anticipating danger not only from criminal acts, but also those which are natural, accidental or unintentional.

    (ii) To safeguard the liberties of the individual and preserve the public peace by seeking to create and maintain conditions under which people may go about their lawful affairs undisturbed and protected from harmful and dangerous conduct.

    (iii) To detect offenders if crime is committed or attempted.

(b) To help every agency having a special community responsibility to seek, identify and eliminate the causes of crime and disorder.

(c) To encourage and advise members of the community on how to protect their persons and property from criminal behaviour; and to mobilise the community in a collaborative effort at prevention and detection of crime.

(d) To study the built-in social mechanisms that normally contribute towards the objective of a peaceful and crime-free society and, where necessary, promote community action and an inter-professional approach to alleviate detected weaknesses in these.

(e) To provide guidance and assistance to anyone who needs

help, especially in cases of tragedy, or family and/or other personal crisis.

(f) To work continuously towards creating a public opinion in favour of both law observance and co-operation with the police.

This definition of the police role has a number of important and apparently novel features. It is stated in a positive way to depict police as aids in protecting democratic society. A collaborative approach to the maintenance of law and order, which also recognises the importance of community co-operation in effective police service, is stressed. The responsibility of the police to use discretion and to endeavour to act in accordance with community values are recognised. The non-criminal activities which police are heavily engaged in are evident in the role definition. Police, more so than any other group in society, are actively and constantly involved in helping to protect the human, civil and individual rights of all citizens. This aspect needs to be reflected in the definition. That police effectiveness in a democracy is largely dependent on public co-operation is undeniable. Therefore, the definition of the police role would be deficient if the vital responsibility of police to secure public confidence were omitted.

A CONCLUDING NOTE

Throughout this essay I have attempted to present a composite picture of the New Zealand police role in its relationship to a changing democratic society. I have tried to make that picture realistic—but with some realisation of Vicker's warning: ". . . Even for the sane, reality is no less an artifact than a fact. The sanest like the maddest of us, cling like spiders to a self-spun web, obscurely moored in vacancy and fiercely shaken by the winds of change."[4]

My underlying aim throughout was to provide insights into an occupation which has been warped by society's expectations and

---

[4] Geoffrey Vickers, *Value Systems and Social Process* (Penguin Books Ltd, London, 1968), p. 197.

prejudices, and to help in clearing a weedy path for bringing police and public even closer together in a teamwork relationship. The policeman standing alone has little influence. When he stands as part of the New Zealand community he commands the support and co-operation of many. The more support he has, the more effective he is in helping to make New Zealanders feel safe and secure.

At the same time, he can only do so much. Indeed, if people see, as I am sure they do, no acceptable alternative to democracy, then it is essential that they also appreciate the importance of policing themselves and that the policeman can do no more than help them in this—he cannot do it for them.

Bibliography

Royal Commission on the Police (London: H.M.S.O., 1962).

Schein, E. H., *Organisational Psychology*, 2nd edition, (Prentice Hall, Inc., 1970).

Etzioni, A., *Modern Organisations* (Prentice Hall, Inc., 1964).

Report of the Canadian Committee on Corrections (Queen's Printer, Ottawa, 31 March 1969).

Knudten, R. D., *Crime in a Complex Society: An Introduction to Criminology* (Illinois, The Dorsey Press, 1970).

Keith, K. J. (ed.), *Essays on Human Rights* (Wellington: Sweet and Maxwell (N.Z.) Ltd., 1968).

President's Commission on Law Enforcement and Administration of Justice. Task Force Report: The Police (Washington D.C.: Government Printing Office, 1967).

Skolnick, J. H., *Justice Without Trial: Law Enforcement in a Democratic Society* (New York: John Wiley & Sons, 1966).

Wilson, J. D., *Varieties of Police Behaviour: The Management of Law and Order in Eight Communities* (Cambridge: Harvard University Press, 1968).

Kaufman, H., *The Forest Ranger: A Study in Administrative Behaviour* (Baltimore: The John Hopkins Press, 1967).

Vollmer, A., *The Police in Modern Society* (Maryland: McGrath Publishing Co., 1936).

The Rule of Law: An Alternative to Violence, Report of the National Commission on the Causes and Prevention of Violence (Nashville: Aurora Publishers, 1970).

Niederhoffer, A., *Beyond the Shield: The Police in Urban Society* (N.Y.: Doubleday, 1967).

Chevigny, P., *Police Power: Police Abuses in New York City* (N.Y.: Pantheon Books, 1969).

Report of the National Advisory Commission on Civil Disorders (Washington, D.C.: Government Printing Office, 1968).

Crime in the Community: A Survey of Penal Policy in New Zealand (Wellington: Government Printer, 1964).

Crime in New Zealand: A Survey of New Zealand Criminal Behaviour (Wellington: Government Printer, 1968).

Bloch, H. A. and Geis, G. (2nd ed.) *Man, Crime and Society* (New York: Random House, 1970).

Endleman, S. (ed.), *Violence in the Streets: An Analysis of the Distructive Impulses of Society* (London: Gerald Duckworth, 1969).

Ward, P., and Woods, G., *Law and Order in Australia* (Sydney: Angus and Robertson, 1972).

Jones, H., *Crime in a Changing Society* (Penguin Books, 1965).

Law and Order in Canadian Democracy (Ottawa: Government Printing Office, 1949).

Moore, W. E., *Social Change* (Prentice-Hall, 1963).

Toffler, A., *Future Shock* (London: The Bodley Head Ltd, 1970).

Bayley, D. H. and Mendelsohn, H., *Minorities and the Police: Confrontation in America* (N.Y.: The Free Press, 1968).

Reisman, D., *The Lonely Crowd* (New Haven: Yale University Press, 1950).

Perrow, C., *Organisational Analysis: A Sociological View.* (California, Wadsworth Publishing Co. Inc., 1970).

Dynamic Administration: The Collected Papers of Mary Parker Follett (London: Sir Isaac Pitman & Sons Ltd., 1941).

Fry, M., *Arm of the Law* (London: Victor Gollancz Ltd., 1951).

Leinwad, G. (ed.), *Crime and Juvenile Delinquency* (N.Y.: Pocket Books, 1968).

Howard, G., *Guardian's of the Queen's Peace* (London: Odhams Press, 1953).

Rice, A. K., *The Enterprise and its Environment* (London: Tavistock Publications, 1963).

Berkley, G. E., *The Administrative Revolution: Notes on the Passing of Organisational Man* (Prentice Hall, Inc., N.J., 1971).

Berkley, G. E., *The Democratic Policeman* (Boston: Beacon Press 1969).

Whitaker, Ben., *Police* (London: Eyre & Spottiswoode, 1964).

Mosher, F. C., *Democracy and the Public Service* (N.Y.: Oxford University Press, 1968).

Morris, Norval & Hawkins, Gordon, *The Honest Politician's Guide to Crime Control* (University of Chicago Press, 1970).

Martin, Roscoe C., *Grass Roots* (2nd ed.) (University of Alabama Press, 1964).

Jackson, R. M., *Enforcing the Law* (Penguin Books Ltd., 1967).

Rolph, C. H., *Common Sense about Crime and Punishment* (London: Victor Gollancz Ltd., 1961).

Waldo, Dwight, *The Administrative State* (New York: The Ronald Press, 1948).

MacIver, R. M., *The Modern State* (London: Oxford University Press, 1926).

Friedrich, Carl J., *Authority* (Nomas 1) (Harvard University Press, Cambridge, 1958).

Lindsay, A. D., *The Modern Democratic State* (Oxford University Press, London, 1943).

Preiss, Jack J. and Ehrlich, H. J., *An Examination of Role Theory: The Case of the State Police* (University of Nebraska Press, 1966).

Brandstatter, A. F. and Radelpet, L. A. (eds.), *Police and Community Relations: A Source Book* (California: Glencoe Press, 1968).

Westley, William A., *Violence and the Police: A Sociological Study of Law, Custom and Morality* (Massachusetts, Institute of Technology, 1970).

Lambert, John R., *Crime, Police, and Race Relations* (London: Oxford University Press, 1970).

Neiderhoffer, A. and Blumberg, A., *The Ambivalent Force: Perspectives on the Police* (New York: Ginn & Co., 1970).

Quinney, R., *The Social Reality of Crime* (Boston: Little, Brown & Co., 1970).

Clark, R. S. (ed.), *Essays on Criminal Law in New Zealand* (Wellington: Sweet and Maxwell (NZ) Ltd., 1971).

Stretcher, V. G., *The Environment of Law Enforcement* (Prentice Hall, Englewood Cliffs, N.J., 1971).

Bennis, Warren G. and Slater, P. E., *The Temporary Society* (N.Y.: Harper & Rowe, 1968).

Vickers, Geoffrey, *Social Systems and Social Process* (Penguin Books Ltd., 1968).

Timms, Noel, *Roles and Relationships* (London: Routledge and Kegan Paul, 1969).

Task Force Report: The Challenge of Crime in a Free Society (Washington: Government Printing Office, 1967).

Marshall, Geoffrey, *Police and Government* (London: Butler and Tanner Ltd., 1965).

Clark, Ramsay, *Crime in America* (New York: Simon and Schuster, 1970).

Halcomb, Richard L., *The Police and the Public* (Illinois: Charles C. Thomas, 1967).

Lohman, Joseph D., *The Police and Minority Groups* (Chicago Police, 1947).

Rolph, C. H., *The Police and the Public* (London: Heinemann, 1962).

Banton, Michael, *The Police in the Community* (London: Tavistock Publications, 1964).

Ashenhurst, Paul H., *Police and the People* (Illinois: Charles C. Thomas, 1957).

Bordua, David J. (ed.), *The Police: Six Sociological Essays* (New York: Wiley and Sons, 1967).

Seigel, Arthur I. (*et al.*), *Professional Police Human Relations Training* (Illinois: Charles C. Thomas, 1963).

Wilson, O. W., *Police Administration* (New York: McGraw-Hill, Inc., 1963).

Coffey, Eldefonso, Hartinger, *Human Relations* (Englewood Cliffs, Prentice Hall Inc., N.J.: 1971).

Adams, Thomas F., *Law Enforcement: An introduction to the Police Role in the Community* (Prentice Hall Inc., Englewood Cliffs, N.J., 1971).

Dahl, Robert A., *A Preface to Democratic Theory* (Chicago, 1963).
Reith, Charles, *The Blind Eye of History* (London, 1952).
Clark, Donald E., Chapman, A. B. and S., *A Forward Step: Educational Background for Police* (New York, 1966).
Chappell, Duncan and Wilson, P. R., *The Police and Public in Australia and New Zealand* (Queensland: University of Queensland Press 1969).

PERIODICALS (*Various*)
Journal of Criminal Law Criminology and Police Science (U.S.).
Issues in Criminology (U.S.).
Australian Police Journal.
Police Review (U.K.).
The Police Journal (U.K.).
Criminal Law Review (U.K.).
The Police Chief (U.S.).
Annals of the American Academy of Political and Social Science.
Public Administration Review (U.S.).
New Zealand Journal of Public Administration.
New Society (U.K.).
American Sociological Review.
Journal of Social Issues (U.S.).
Journal of Social Problems (U.S.).
The Sociological Quarterly (U.S.).
The New Zealand Social Worker.
The Nation (U.S.).
American Sociological Review.